THE ART OF
ANTHONY TROLLOPE

THE ART OF
ANTHONY
TROLLOPE

Geoffrey Harvey

ST. MARTIN'S PRESS
New York

Sections of this book originally appeared in slightly
different form in *ARIEL, Wascana Review, Texas
Studies in Literature and Language, Studies in
English Literature*, and the *Yearbook of English
Studies*.

Printed in Great Britain
First published in the United States of America in
1980

Library of Congress Cataloging in Publication Data

Harvey, Geoffrey, 1943 –
    The art of Anthony Trollope.

    Bibliography: p.
    Includes index.
    1. Trollope, Anthony, 1815 – 1882—Criticism
and interpretation. I. Title.
PR5687.H3 1980   823'.8   80 – 5088
ISBN 0 – 312 – 04998 – 6

To my Mother and in memory of my Father

CONTENTS

Acknowledgements

I should like to thank the staffs of several libraries for their invaluable assistance: the Brynmor Jones Library of the University of Hull, the Bodleian, the British Library, the Folger Shakespeare Library, Washington, D.C., the John Rylands Library of the University of Manchester, and the Killam Library of Dalhousie University.

I am particularly grateful to Professor Arthur Pollard, who encouraged my study of Trollope in its early stages and offered much timely guidance. Thanks are also due to my former colleagues at Dalhousie University, especially Dr Allan Bevan and Dr Gary Waller, for their lively and critical interest in my work. More recently I have received encouragement from my colleagues at Bulmershe College of Higher Education, notably Dennis Butts, and I am indebted to Christine MacLeod for her meticulous reading of my manuscript. Nevertheless, I am of course solely responsible for what follows.

Parts of this book have appeared in a slightly different form in the following journals: *ARIEL* (1975), *Wascana Review* (1975), *Texas Studies in Literature and Language* (1976), *Studies in English Literature* (1976) and the *Yearbook of English Studies* (1979). I am grateful to the editors and to the Board of Governors of the University of Calgary, the University of Saskatchewan, the University of Texas Press, William Marsh Rice University and the Modern Humanities Research Association for permission to reprint.

Finally I wish to record my gratitude to my wife and family for suffering my work on Trollope with such patience.

A Note on References

Since there is no standard or complete edition of Trollope's works, quotations from the novels and the *Autobiography* are taken from the Oxford World's Classics editions, as being those most readily available to the reader, with the exception of *An Eye for An Eye*, which was published by Anthony Blond (London, 1966). Where these are double volume editions, I have indicated parenthetically in my text both the page and volume numbers.

The following abbreviations are used throughout the notes for works cited frequently:

An Autobiography	Anthony Trollope, *An Autobiography*, (Oxford, World's Classics, 1953, reprinted 1961).
Letters	*The Letters of Anthony Trollope*, ed. Bradford A. Booth (London, 1951).
Marginalia	Folger Shakespeare Library, Washington, D.C., Trollope's marginalia in his editions of the early drama.
Papers	Bodleian Library, Oxford, *Trollope*, Papers Relating to His Work, 3 vols., MS. Don. C.9., C.10., C.10*.
Thackeray	Anthony Trollope, *Thackeray* (London, 1879).

I

INTRODUCTION

In spite of their varying estimates of Trollope's fiction and their conflicting interpretations of his individual novels, critics are virtually unanimous about the existence of a 'Trollope problem'. Most obviously there is the strange ambiguity of his position in the critical hierarchy of Victorian novelists, especially when some half dozen of his novels are by any standards first-rate fiction. Then there is the fact that, in contrast to his fellow novelists, we still have no complete edition of his works. However, the major problem facing critics striving to come to grips with this most apparently substantial yet in many ways most elusive of Victorian writers, has been succinctly summarized by C. P. Snow in a perceptive essay on Trollope's craft: 'Trollope wrote so much and, of all writers, he is the one least adapted for most kinds of academic approach. How do you dig into him? And with what books?'[1] What critics have tended to do is to construct their own Trollope, dipping into his many novels according to their own particular interests. And the Trollopes so created are many and varied – the entertainer, the psychological writer, the moralist, the political novelist, and the social historian. This present study is no exception and in it I propose to discuss my own Trollope: Trollope the artist.

As C. P. Snow intimates, the central question is whether Trollope is accessible to standard critical procedures, for he is not a symbolic or poetic novelist, nor a novelist of ideas, nor indeed a technical innovator in any obvious sense. However, James R. Kincaid, who is optimistic that we now have a criticism capable of dealing with Trollope, believes that 'the growing strength of formalist and structuralist criticism may spring Trollope from the historicist trap in which even his admirers had placed him'.[2] But is it really necessary or useful to 'spring' Trollope from the 'historicist trap'? I do not believe that it is; for perhaps more than any other English novelist Trollope is truly representative of his age, as regards both his choice of material and the form of his fiction. My intention is to show how his art draws its strength from its roots in the Victorian ethos and particularly from the critical debates on the form of the novel which were current during the peak of his writing career.

A fundamental aspect of the 'Trollope problem' is the fact that his personality and his literary career possessed many curious features. His fiction exerted a fascination over the intellectual and the common reader alike. Not only was he admired by such distinguished writers as George Eliot, Henry James, Tolstoy and Shaw, but, as R. C. Terry reminds us, he was a continuing favourite with readers who subscribed to Charles Mudie's great circulating library, which dominated English middle-class reading habits. Indeed Trollope was read quite widely until well into this century, reaching a peak of popularity around 1900.[3] More interesting perhaps, is the contradiction between the man and his novels. 'Some of Trollope's acquaintances', remarks Frederick Locker-Lampson, 'used to wonder how so commonplace a person could have written such excellent novels'.[4] Indeed, several of his contemporaries commented on the dichotomy between the ebullient, fox-hunting extrovert and the subtle, often coolly ironic novelist. In public Trollope was a magnetic, vital, popular figure, but in private he was extremely reticent, even in his correspondence. And this habitual reserve was not broken even in his *Autobiography* which, if anything, deepens rather than elucidates the mystery. Indeed, he asserts quite bluntly that he has deliberately omitted giving us a record of his inner life.[5] And as far as his art is concerned, his references are exasperatingly casual because, as he claimed jocularly, he did not believe that he would be read into the next century.[6] The truth is, I think, that the *Autobiography* is really a very defensive document. It was commenced in 1867, the year of Trollope's greatest popularity after the enormous success of *The Last Chronicle of Barset*, and was written almost as a way of explaining to himself his amazing good fortune and of justifying his chosen profession. So it serves to perpetuate the paradoxes: the discrepancy between Trollope's treatment of his novels as marketable goods and his desire to vindicate his calling by writing a history of the novel, and between the cavalier way he refers to his own work and the care and discipline he advocates to everyone who asks his advice about writing.

Self-doubt goes a long way towards explaining why Trollope took such pains to conceal his indisputable commitment to his art. His defensiveness, both as a man and as an artist, can be traced to his childhood. There were the three miserable years at Harrow from the age of seven until his tenth year, where he felt awkward and disreputable because of his stupidity, his shyness and the poverty of his dress, and where the feeling was impressed upon him that he would never manage to succeed like his fellow pupils.[7] Then followed a period of utter friendlessness at Winchester College while his family moved to Cincinnati, and a shame-faced return to Harrow, this time as an even shabbier boy, when the family fortunes declined. Self-distrust became engrained in him during this desolate time of his life. Like Dickens, he was a gentleman's son who was not treated as such by his school-fellows. He felt isolated and intensely lonely, and it was during this period, as he reveals in his *Autobiography*, that he escaped into a private world of make-believe which became the foundation of his later writing. And these sad, enervating years were followed by an equally desperate period as an usher in a school in Brussels (where his duties included teaching classics to thirty boys) until, following the deaths of his brother, his father and his sister, he was sent in 1834 at the age of nineteen to work in London as a junior clerk at the General Post Office. We learn very little from the *Autobiography* about this period, which lasted seven long years; however Trollope's treatment of young men living in London in *The Three Clerks*, *The Small House at Allington*, *Phineas Finn* and *Ralph the Heir* presents a cumulative picture of intense loneliness, uncertainty and lack of purpose.

3

Even though Trollope himself is reticent about them, we should not underestimate the effect on him of these early experiences. One obvious consequence was the fact that when success finally overtook him in the 1860s he grasped it firmly and enjoyed it to the full. During this decade he had twenty novels in various stages of publication. He also cooperated with Thackeray on the *Cornhill*, founded the *Fortnightly Review*, wrote plays and essays, was elected Chairman of the Garrick Club Committee, stood for Parliament, and acquired many friends highly placed in the professions and in London literary circles. The assaults made on his self-respect during his boyhood had served to nurture his ambition. When the opportunity presented itself he endeavoured to succeed in a wide field of activities – in the public service, writing, politics, editing and amateur scholarship. But the habit of self-deprecation, which was deeply engrained in him, was intensified rather than assuaged by success. The more triumphant he was, the more fragile his success seemed, and the more vulnerable he felt. This is perhaps best illustrated by Frederic Harrison's anecdote about Trollope describing his method of work to a gathering at George Eliot's home. Trollope and George Eliot were close friends. She respected his writing and indeed revealed that *The Way We Live Now* had given her the courage to persevere with *Middlemarch*. But she was an intellectual and Trollope was not. Because he felt intimidated he told his story about writing for three hours every day at the rate of two hundred and fifty words every quarter of an hour. George Eliot replied that there were days when she could not write even a line. " 'Yes', said Trollope, 'with imaginative work like yours that is quite natural; but with my mechanical stuff it's a sheer matter of industry. It's not the head that does it – it's the cobbler's wax on the seat and the sticking to my chair!' "[8]

But if this comment includes a measure of self-denigration as well as admiration for a superior novelist, it also contains a hard-headed realism. Like all professional writers, Trollope was acutely aware that art was only partly inspiration; the rest was hard work, and it is in order to debunk the romantic attitude to writing that he refers to himself crudely as a rustic driving pigs to market.[9] But an important insight into Trollope's under-lying commitment to his art is given by his contemporary T. H. S. Escott, who remarks that '[f]ew writers, perhaps, have taken themselves more in earnest than Trollope'.[10] This is corroborated in Trollope's monograph on his friend Thackeray, which reveals his understanding that a writer possesses special gifts. A man should write a book, he says, 'because it is in him to write it, – the motive power being altogether in himself and coming from his desire to express himself'.[11] *Thackeray* also contains a homely description of the way Trollope himself worked by ceaseless observation and reflection: 'forethought', he affirms, 'is the elbow-grease which a novelist, – or a poet, or dramatist, – requires'.[12] This preparation for writing, the long gestation of characters and incidents, was rooted in the habit of day-dreaming which he had formed in childhood; indeed, in his later years much of his inner life, he tells us, was passed in the company of the Pallisers.[13] And although by his own admission Trollope was primarily a novelist of character, he understood the crucial importance of form. Referring to *Framley Parsonage*, he talks of the power of fitting the beginning to the end,[14] while his criticism of the novel of his young protégée, Kate Field, focuses on the fact that 'the end of [her] story should have been the beginning'.[15]

Of course these comments are not profound criticism. Trollope was not an intellectual critic; he wrote as a practising novelist. And in any case the bluffness of his critical remarks is often part of his defensive mask. However, most accounts of Trollope would have us believe that, although he was the son of a woman who in her day was a famous writer, and despite the fact that he was the close friend of novelists, dramatists and critics like Thackeray, George Eliot, Charles Reade, Bulwer-Lytton, George Henry Lewes, Sir Henry Taylor and Richard Holt Hutton, he was nevertheless a writer who possessed little theoretic con-ception of his art. In this book I am concerned to argue that this view, although abetted by Trollope himself, flies in the face of probability. Trollope knew better than most that art is artificial. Like most other writers he recognized that realism is only a convention, but unlike them he said so unequivocally:

'And yet in very truth the realistic must not be true – but just so far removed from truth as to suit the erroneous idea of truth which the reader may be supposed to entertain'.[16] Realism for Trollope is 'that which shall seem to be real'.[17] It should not surprise us then, that his art is altogether a more subtle and a more conscious business than his own cobbling metaphor suggests, or than critics have believed. However, in spite of the recent remarkable rise of critical interest in Trollope, the image of him as a rather pedestrian writer somehow persists. The sheer quantity, bulk and comprehensiveness of his writing throughout his career means that the form of his novels has not been given sufficiently serious critical attention. His work is too often equated with the study of the surface of social life, with the conventional or accidental ending, with lack of finesse in plotting and construction, with a garrulous interest in character and with padding and irrelevance. But the form of Trollope's novels is a striking aspect of his art, and it is his scrupulous concern with this area of his writing that forms the substance of this present study. And not art simply in the narrow formal sense, but also as an expression of the conventions within which the Victorian novelist wrote. Far from believing that Trollope needs to be rescued from the 'historicist trap', in my view the sheer complexity of the artistic achievement in his major novels can only be understood by a careful consideration of his art within the immediate historical context of contemporary critical theory.

The form of Trollope's novels encompasses both his moral vision of the world and his communication of it to the reader. It may thus be regarded as a relation between moral vision, structure and effect, which corresponds to the relation between author, novel and reader and which expresses that relation within the novel itself. Briefly then, Trollope's created 'world' and its expression inhere in the novel by means of form. It may be objected that my use of the term 'form' is too imprecise to be useful, but I hope that the following discussion and my reading of the individual novels will amplify and define it further. Of course there are many different aspects of form, just as there are many facets of vision and methods of communication, but those which Trollope employs with consumate skill seem to me, considering the weight of both internal and external evidence, to derive mainly from the major formal conventions within which the Victorian novelist worked: the drama, the omniscient author and the serial mode of publication.

The influence of the drama on the art of such novelists as Dickens, Wilkie Collins and Charles Reade is, of course, well known. But its impact on the form of the Victorian novel was more pervasive than that. As S. W. Dawson has put it: 'it was not until the nineteenth century that the possibility arose of a dramatic form capable of surpassing the drama of the theatre in depth and vitality'.[18] It is significant, I think, that almost without exception the major as well as the minor novelists nursed an ambition to succeed in the theatre. Nearly all of them wrote plays, many of which achieved public performance. However, because the best of these writers felt the urgent need to give artistic expression to the dynamic thrust of social change in mid-Victorian England, they discovered that the only appropriate form for their work was the expansive form of the novel rather than the restricted form of the drama. This is immediately evident when we examine Trollope's own writing and compare the sweeping social panorama of *The Last Chronicle of Barset* with the cramped, stilted play *Did He Steal It?*, which he boiled down from the novel; or the maturity of moral insight and social observation apparent in *Can You Forgive Her?* which is so sadly absent from the earlier play *The Noble Jilt*, on which it is partly based. Trollope fully shared the Victorian writers' ambition for success in the theatre, and in spite of the fact that his two plays were still-born he nevertheless remained fascinated by the drama and was greatly stimulated by the contemporary critical debate about the possibility of creating a genuinely dramatic form in the novel. As a consequence, in the 1860s while at the peak of his fame, Trollope succumbed to the temptation to experiment that resulted in his astonishing production of a series of anonymous novels. Brief, single-plotted works, each is prefaced by a list of dramatis personae and falls into three well defined 'acts'. Moreover, each possesses dramatic compression and intensity together with a sense of closure and completion, and Trollope clearly aims at the creation of a tragic, fatalistic world. However, his multi-plotted novels, which gained much greater maturity and artistic control during this decade, are also rooted formally in the drama, in this case the ampler conventions employed by the Jacobeans. In these novels the subsidiary plots form an ironic or even cynical counterpoint to the main plot, and the pattern is open-ended. Characters are given more freedom, life is less predictable and the action displays greater social complexity. This more flexible form supports the moral articulation of the novels in an unobtrusive way, not only because it takes hundreds of pages to work itself through, but also because it is embedded in the density of realistic detail. These novels too, in short, possess a far greater formal coherence than critics have recognized.

The narrative or rhetorical element in the mid-Victorian novel largely meant, at least for most contemporary critics and reviewers, the presence of the writer's authentic voice. And although some of the great Victorian novelists might be described as dramatists *manqués*, they saw themselves primarily as storytellers for whom the use of an authorial persona was particularly important. It is most evident in Dickens, George Eliot and Thackeray as well as in Trollope, but its widespread employment had, by the 1860s, become the focus of a fierce debate between those critics who favoured the dramatic form of the novel, which meant the virtual exclusion of the author (one might perhaps call them pre-Jamesian Jamesians) and those who, like George Eliot and Trollope especially, felt that the novel should tell a story. Those who championed the dramatic form, like George Henry Lewes, for instance, did so in the interests of greater artistic unity and formal realism. However, as moralists, George Eliot and Trollope agreed that the novel also had a clear ethical purpose which demanded a peculiar rhetoric of its own.[19] But Trollope made his rhetoric serve ends which were not merely moral but also mimetic and artistic. He made the garrulous, intrusive voice of the author the basis of his realism. In his manifold references to work, social and cultural institutions, leisure pursuits, moral attitudes and the like Trollope's narrative voice builds into the novel

8

those laws by which its world operates, laws similar to those in the real world, in order to convince the reader of its truth without his having to refer outside the novel itself. This use of the author's voice is obviously very different from Dickens's great poetic, atmospheric set pieces, which draw the reader compellingly into the novel until he is no longer aware of its contiguity with the real-world. However, although Trollope does achieve the fictional illusion of a self-contained world offered for our involvement, at the same time his numerous asides to the reader, sometimes witty, often cynically deflating, frequently inviting collaboration with the author, are concerned to remind us that art is only art, that fiction is merely fiction. Yet he rarely does so in such a way as to destroy the powerful illusion of reality that he has already achieved. And the effect is plainly moral. It prevents us from becoming too sympathetically immersed in the story, detaching us so that we can also judge its characters, their actions and their world. More importantly, by thus sustaining a profound tension between our imaginative sympathy and our moral scrutiny, Trollope asserts the need for moral relativism, for the necessity to attend scrupulously to the situation of the individual and the pressures exerted by his environment. It is essentially a fluid and open form which encourages us to seek a moral evaluation of the pattern of life presented to us, while reminding us that art is not life and that what we see as pattern may be neither whole nor wholly true. In short, we are enjoined to exercise our moral discrimination at the highest level.

Many mid-Victorian novelists such as Thackeray and the early Dickens for instance, were charged by contemporary reviewers with a formal slackness which was often laid at the door of the hectic convention of serial publication. The novelists' obligation to their public was made more onerous by the proliferation of magazines in the 1860s, each of which carried an instalment of at least one novel. It was a system which encouraged authors to write hand to mouth, and it tended moreover to foster a garrulous intimacy with the reading public. More seriously, the serial convention dictated a form which was rigid, mechanical and which aimed at moving the reader's emotions by a pattern of backward glance and rising intonation, by sensational action followed by curtain-line endings in order to secure suspense and excitement. Rhetorical in the worst sense, it militated against realism, especially the subtle moral realism which was Trollope's particular mode.

As Trollope makes clear in his *Autobiography*, he was well aware of these pitfalls even before he came to write his first serialized novel, *Framley Parsonage*, and he was determined to overcome them. Characteristically, because he is such a careful artist, Trollope achieves much more than that. By paying close attention to the unity and coherence of the serial part, by articulating formal patterns in the novel as a whole and by a judicious use of the author's voice, he creates a series of mnemonic devices which keep the world of the novel and the author's moral view in the reader's mind, achieving in each episode a sense of aesthetic completion together with the tension of foreshadowed development and a feeling of continuity. Thus in Trollope's hands even this obstinate convention is transformed into an art. Its pattern is given greater flexibility and possesses the rhetorical function of continually directing the reader's attention to the wider context of the writer's vision, while also serving our sense of realism, for it parallels our own intermittent apprehension of other people's lives as a continuing serial which we pick up and put down with fluctuating interest as they appear from time to time on our narrow horizons.

Trollope possesses the artistic ability to make a daring extension of the traditional novel conventions because his imagination is a powerful synthesizing force, holding in significant tension these separate aspects of the novel's form. The consequence for his fiction is an art which contains both the pattern and the inconsequentiality of life, the density of a fully realized social world together with the moral and psychological centrality of character. Of course this complex synthesis could only be fully revealed by an exhaustive and, to a certain extent, repetitive and even tedious analysis of a single novel. What I have opted to do instead is to examine these aspects of form separately in those splendid novels, *The Last Chronicle of Barset* and *Orley Farm*, in the fascinating experimental and anonymous works, *Nina Balatka* and *An Eye for An Eye,* and in the excellent and underrated novel, *The Claverings.* I conclude with a more general assessment of Trollope's major achievement in *The Way We Live Now* and *The Prime Minister.* My historical interest in the influences on Trollope's art is reflected in the way each chapter outlines the essential, immediate context of mid-Victorian critical debate on the novel. However, the greatest emphasis in this book falls on Trollope's uses of the drama and these chapters include, together with an examination of the nature of his debts to his vast reading in the Jacobean drama, a detailed account of his employment of the dramatic form in several major novels.

I ought also to explain why, unlike most recent critics, I have not chosen to deal with the bulk of Trollope's fiction, or with his development as a novelist. As my selection of novels indicates, this study is principally concerned with Trollope's writing in the 1860s and early 1870s. There are several reasons for this. Firstly, as the novelist most widely read by the Victorians, Trollope is a fruitful source for the study of generally accepted novel conventions. His contemporary, George Saintsbury, described his popularity thus: 'I do not know that I myself ever took Mr. Trollope for one of the immortals; but really between 1860 and 1870 it might have been excusable so to take him'.[20] And more recently Kenneth Graham has called him the 'High Priest of Victorian realism'.[21] Secondly, it was during this period that the formal conventions of the novel were first seriously discussed and, as David Skilton has demonstrated, Trollope's work naturally became the focus of this debate.[22] The third reason is that, in my view, the period spanning roughly 1860–75, coming after those years in which Trollope struggled to make his reputation with *Barchester Towers* and to consolidate it with the success of *Framley Parsonage,* represents the high-water mark of his writing career, the period during which he matured as a novelist and in which he paid the most serious attention to the practice of his art.

Although I am not really concerned in this book with literary biography, some knowledge of those aspects of Trollope's early life, critical interests and working habits which critics have tended to neglect is essential to a judicious understanding of his art as a novelist and should be given here in brief outline. As Trollope's library catalogue and his prolonged study of Jacobean plays demonstrate, he possessed a profound enthusiasm for the drama.[23] Perhaps it provided an important path back to the memories of amateur theatricals at Julians, the farmhouse near Harrow (later to be the model for Orley Farm) where he experienced probably some of the few bright spots in his solitary and miserable boyhood. Indeed, his family background was steeped in the theatre. His parents shared a particular devotion to Molière, whose works the family enacted, in addition to the usual Renaissance and Restoration drama, in the Julians drawing-room, and later in Brussels, Italy and Cincinnati.[24] Frances Trollope records how Mrs Trollope took her children to see her admired Mlle Mars as Elmire in *Tartuffe* in Paris,[25] and Thomas Trollope notes how the Trollope parents frequently underwent privations in order to appreciate the quality of Mrs Siddons's performance as Lady Macbeth from the pit.[26] Mrs Trollope particularly, threw herself into the world of the theatre, claiming the close friendship of William Charles Macready, Charles Keane, the Kembles, Henry Taylor ('Van Artevelde Taylor' as he was known after his famous historical play) and Mary Russell Mitford.[27] These and others less well known were frequent visitors to Julians, bringing the magical atmosphere of the theatre into the Trollope household.

Trollope's continued interest in the drama is evident during the period 1850–3 when, as his marginalia in his copies of the plays testify, he was engaged in an extensive study of the Jacobean drama and had just completed his first play. His studies recommenced, after a long tour of duty for the Post Office in Ireland, when he returned to London in 1859. The reason, I believe, was the fresh intellectual stimulus which stemmed from success and from new associations. The remarkable popularity of *Framley Parsonage* gained Trollope an invitation to George Smith's first *Cornhill* dinner in 1860. He was well liked and his new circle of friends soon included George Eliot and George Henry Lewes, Edward Bulwer-Lytton, Sir Henry Taylor and Richard Holt Hutton of the *Spectator*. His friendship with

12

Lewes in particular quickly blossomed. Temperamentally they complemented each other, they shared an absorbing interest in acting, the stage and French classical drama, and while Lewes had been impressed by *Barchester Towers*, Trollope greatly admired Lewes as a critic and a theorist.[28] It is not surprising, therefore, that for a time in the 1860s Trollope was torn between the neo-Aristotelian aesthetic, espoused by Lewes and Hutton, which demanded unity and proportion of the dramatic novel, and the Victorian novelist's instinctive desire, as W.C. Roscoe noted, to give expression in a more ample and complex form to his sense of a burgeoning society.[29] This problem was partly solved for Trollope by his meeting with his mother's old friend Sir Henry Taylor who, apart from being a famous playwright himself, nurtured an abiding passion for the Jacobean drama which rekindled Trollope's dormant enthusiasm for further study.[30] This spilled over into his creative life and he gradually perfected a more extensive dramatic form in order to embody the social realism of his panoramic novels.

Another of Mrs Trollope's friends who also took Trollope under his wing on his return to England was Edward Bulwer-Lytton, whose interest, apart from his own novel-writing and the drama, was the theory of the novel.[31] In the early 1860s Bulwer-Lytton was working on a series of articles for *Blackwood's Edinburgh Magazine* within which one finds embedded in embryonic form a theory about the rhetorical interplay of sympathy with irony in the novel as a means of moving the reader's emotions while at the same time stimulating his moral judgement. It is a theory which Trollope repeats almost verbatim in his *Autobiography* and in his essay on prose fiction and which, in my view, he first consciously employed in the novel he was then working on, *Orley Farm*. And as far as the serialization of fiction is concerned, Trollope tells us that by the time he came to write his first serialized novel *Framley Parsonage* for the *Cornhill*, he had learned from the experience of Dickens, Mrs Gaskell and Thackeray, the dangers of writing hand to mouth. He was aware of how it impaired the unity of the novel, how it tempted the author to sensationalize his material; and because he had already thought long about the problem he began to devise his own method of serial construction in the 1860s which came to maturity in his third serialized novel, *The Claverings*.

Although this study is primarily concerned with Trollope's art, I hope it also pays due attention to the intellectual substance of that art, for what a close examination of Trollope's practice as a novelist offers the critic who approaches it from a historicist point of view is a fresh perspective on the nature of his social criticism. For the most part critics have not given Trollope's penetrating critique of Victorian society the degree of serious attention that it deserves. For many, Trollope is still an avuncular, conservative figure and they frequently stress his affection for the rural squirearchy, his love of fox-hunting, his bland amusement at diocesan politics and his approving interest in the workings of the professions and the political world. This judgement is apparently strengthened by his own definition of his political creed as being that of an 'advanced conservative Liberal'.[32] But critics tend to emphasize 'conservative' rather than 'advanced', and regard him as being at his most radical a meliorist like Walter Bagehot with whom he has often been compared.[33] However, if we give due weight to Trollope's artistic statements and read his novels paying strict attention to the way their meaning is expressed by their form, we discover that not only is his criticism of English society and its institutions sharper than Bagehot's, but his support of the gradual movement towards democracy is also stronger. Trollope has a keener sense of the still basically feudal nature of English life and he is impatiently hostile, especially in his later novels, to its blind reverence for tradition, its exclusiveness, the rigidity of its class system and its lack of vision and energy. That his true sympathy is with the democrats is evident not only in his book *North America* in which he expresses his admiration for the new-found social mobility and independence of the labouring man, but in the novels as well, and particularly in his approval of men like Daniel Thwaite, Ontario Moggs, Mr Monk and Plantagenet Palliser. And because I believe that Trollope's attitude towards his world generally is rather more radical than critics have thought, it follows that I think the notion of his progress towards pessimism places the emphasis in the wrong quarter. If one thinks of the overwhelmingly tragic tone of an early novel like *The Macdermots of Ballycloran*, or the sardonic attack on the Civil Service in *The Three Clerks*, his satirical analysis of the legal system and its values in *Orley Farm*, his disenchanted view of bourgeois marriage in *The Claverings*, his condemnation of clerical politics in *The Last Chronicle of Barset*, quite apart from the heavy satire and profound pessimism of *The Way We Live Now* and *The Prime Minister*, it is clear that throughout his writing career Trollope possessed, in addition to the comic impulse, a mature, disenchanted vision of the Victorian world.

The appropriate place, it seems to me, to begin to seek the basis of Trollope's social criticism is at that point where the creative process is triggered into activity. And in this respect we are fortunate in knowing something of the extent to which he drew imaginatively on his vast reading in the Jacobean drama. Although, as C. J. Vincent has pointed out, Trollope is in a sense a Victorian Augustan, an heir to the tradition of Jane Austen and Fielding, he can equally be described with some justice as a Victorian Jacobean.[34] Although he was acutely aware of the limitations and absurdities of much of the drama, he discovered affinities with certain dramatists which reveal his cast of mind as having a good deal in common with Middleton and Fletcher – with Middleton's critique of city life and with Fletcher's concern for the individual. Moreover, like theirs, his realism always has a sharp cutting-edge, even in sunny novels like *Barchester Towers* or *The Small House at Allington*, which appear to sanction Victorian morals and manners. Like Middleton, his criticism is directed mainly at the middle classes, at their snobbery, conservatism, greed, hypocrisy and prejudice. Trollope makes the most comprehensive survey of middle-class life that we have in our literature because he wanted to explain to his fellow-Victorians why their society was not as healthy as they pretended. He examines those areas in which real power is vested – the Church, the law, the Civil Service, Parliament, the city and the squirearchy. Although controlled for the most part by ordinary, well-meaning men, as institutions they take on a life of their own. They seek to retain power in the hands of a privileged few and are dedicated with a ferocious though genteel intensity to preserving the *status quò*. That is why Trollope is always on the side of the outsider, even when, like Ferdinand Lopez, he is morally reprehensible. He is concerned to explore those situations in which isolated individuals like Mr Crawley, Miss Mackenzie, Lady Mason, or Lopez threaten the establishment, and in doing so he reveals the frighteningly uniform façade which society presents in its efforts to crush opposition and to preserve cherished illusions, such as the ideals of heroism, Christian faith, social mobility, justice, or the sanctity of hearth and home. These rest upon a fragile social consensus and their defence, Trollope demonstrates, is a process which results in the continual assumption of masks and the dangerous erosion of human individuality.

However, Trollope eschews absolutes. Even when he is at his most satirical, he recognizes much that is praiseworthy in the values of English life and traditions and has faith in the simple goodness of fallible people. His belief in the supreme value of the individual and his right to self-determination demands a moral relativism which makes allowances for the special case and for the intense pressures of a rapidly changing social environment. His fiction therefore encompasses contradiction as the finest realism should, and it is this refusal to reduce his vision of the world, this determination to preserve its multi-faceted quality, that gives to Trollope's novels their unique authenticity.

II
TROLLOPE AND
THE DRAMA

Trollope and the Jacobean Drama

TROLLOPE'S public reputation as one of the foremost exponents of realism in the Victorian novel and his private addiction to the Jacobean drama create an intriguing paradox; but even more fascinating is the influence of these plays on his writing of the novels. The parallels of moral and social pattern are partly due to Trollope's recognition of tensions in his own burgeoning society similar to those evident in the rapidly changing Jacobean world; and the Jacobean dramatists employ several socio-moral themes – the redemption of the prodigal, the impoverishment of the gentry by the rising merchant class, the scrutiny of aristocratic values, the newly subversive spirit of the independent wealthy woman and the testing of the response of feminine virtue to altered social conditions – which reappear in the novels that I wish to discuss in this section: *The Three Clerks, Miss Mackenzie, Ralph the Heir, Lady Anna, The Fixed Period* and *The Prime Minister*. However, the parallels between the plays and the novels are more than simply a general affinity of artistic interests. Since Trollope read and annotated 257 early plays, it is highly probable that some direct borrowing occurred. Indeed, he admits as much in his *Autobiography*: 'How far I may unconsciously have adopted incidents from what I have read, – either from history or from works of imagination, – I do not know. It is beyond question that a man employed as I have been must do so. But when doing it I have not been aware that I have done it'.[1] Moreover, his statement: 'I have found my greatest pleasure in our old English dramatists, – not from any excessive love of their work . . . but from curiosity in searching their plots and examining their characters'[2] suggests the strong likelihood of some specific indebtedness and in two instances at least, as Bradford Booth has demonstrated, Trollope's debts range from verbal echoes of Marlowe's *Doctor Faustus* in *Orley Farm* to his adoption of the plot of *The Old Law*, by Massinger, Middleton and Rowley in *The Fixed Period*.[3]

Surprisingly, in those novels under discussion Trollope does not conflate an amalgam of situations, plots and characters drawn from his immense reading in the Jacobean drama, but rather, with one exception, each novel displays his indebtedness to a particular play which gripped his imagination and which rose to the surface when he was groping for a piece of characterization, an embryonic plot, the development of a theme, or a unifying pattern. Since Trollope was studying the drama rather than poetry, apart from *Doctor Faustus* there are no verbal reminiscences, to clinch the matter of his borrowing. And moreover, although in the case of *The Prime Minister* his marginalia dating of Fletcher's *Women Pleased* offers corroborative evidence, for the most part Trollope's dating is of little assistance because it frequently records that he was reading the play for the fourth or fifth time. It is necessary, therefore, to look beyond verbal echoes, marginalia dating and the socio-moral themes which the plays and novels share, to similarities of characterization, parallels of situation, of plot development, emblematic pattern, the echo of characters' names, or to the presence in the novel of extraneous incidents which indicate a debt to a specific play. Indeed, the closeness of these parallels in the novels that I discuss puts Trollope's borrowing, I think, beyond doubt and reveals that his debts are more extensive than scholars have realized. The evidence also suggests, at least in the case of some novels, that they are more conscious than Trollope recalled them as having been when he wrote the *Autobiography*. It seems likely that with the passage of time his debts had faded from his memory of the novels, although they obviously lingered in the back of his mind.[4] Trollope found the whole ethos of the Jacobean drama a reflection of his own society and its problems. He was fascinated by the parallels that he observed between the social tensions of the Jacobean world and the Victorian class struggle : the similar intensification of economic and social competition, the waning of the aristocracy, the concomitant rise of the wealthy bourgeoisie and the emergence of a dominant middle-class ethic. But it was particular plays which provided the immediate catalysts for the operation of his imagination. Because Trollope did not simply transcribe the material that he adopted, an examination of the process of creative transformation affords us an insight not only into his artistic methods but into the shaping of his social criticism. Although John H. Hagan has described Trollope's mind as politically 'divided',[5] Trollope's treatment of the material that he borrowed from the Jacobean drama offers evidence that the true instinct of his mind was more radical than has been thought, and in those novels on which I wish to focus attention he anatomizes the moral anarchy that he felt lay just below the bland surface of middle and upper class Victorian society.

Trollope's *The Three Clerks* is more than merely a collection of comic autobiographical sketches of his early years as a post office clerk in the London of the eighteen thirties. Its prodigal son motif, developed in the parallel careers of the junior Civil Service clerks, derives from the contrasted careers of the apprentices in the satiric city comedy *Eastward Ho!* by Jonson, Chapman and Marston. Despite the fact that the structure of both the play and the novel is a very natural socio-moral pattern, there are a series of close parallels between them of characterization, structure, situation and incident. Alaric and Charley Tudor owe a great deal to the character of Quicksilver, an ambitious scapegrace; the puritanical clerk Henry Norman is modelled on the doggedly virtuous apprentice, Golding; and the goldsmith's daughters Gertrude and Mildred appear in the novel as Gertrude and Linda Woodward. A typical city comedy woman of the citizen class, Gertrude Touchstone's monomaniacal desire for social elevation, fostered by her weak-minded mother, finds a parallel in the intense social ambition of the Gertrude of the novel. There is a further parallel of situation between the marriage of Gertrude Touchstone and the impoverished gentleman Sir Petronel Flash, who seeks to gain her estate and Gertrude Woodward's match with the penniless Alaric Tudor, who wants her legacy. And in contrast, Mildred's dutiful acquiescence in her father's choice of his sober apprentice for her husband is paralleled in the novel by the virtuous Linda Woodward's passive acceptance of Henry Norman, a marriage which, like Gertrude's, is planned quietly by Mrs Woodward, whose sententious moralizing strikes a key note throughout the novel and who thus subsumes the functions of both Touchstone and his wife in the play.

The play's central, overt debate between prodigality and prudence, advanced on the one hand by the rascally apprentice Quicksilver and Touchstone's ambitious daughter Gertrude, and on the other by his virtuous apprentice Golding and his righteous daughter Mildred, is also fundamental to the clear moral design of *The Three Clerks*, in which the schematic moral contrast between the prudent clerk Henry Norman and his ambitious friend Alaric Tudor, who is 'no Puritan' immediately recalls the parallel of characterization in *Eastward Ho!*. Like Quicksilver, Tudor is frustrated by bourgeois values of thrift, industry and respectability and just as the Jacobean apprentice's social climbing is aided by money stolen from Touchstone, the Victorian clerk, who covets a seat in Parliament, advances his meteoric career by the theft of his ward's fortune. In both the play and the novel the criminals are tried and imprisoned, both repenting their folly, while the moralists, who preach to them while paying off their debts, are rewarded appropriately, Golding being elected a city alderman, while Norman inherits a country estate.

There are also further minor parallels of various kinds which give vitality and point to different areas of the novel. Quicksilver, for instance, also serves as a model for the third clerk Charley Tudor, the 'prodigal', who is reclaimed, like the apprentice, only after falling into the clutches of a money-lender and suffering temporary imprisonment. Indeed, he only narrowly escapes Quicksilver's fate. Quicksilver marries his whore, whose dowry is paid by the usurer Security, while Tudor nearly marries the barmaid of the 'Cat and Whistle', Trollope's Victorian equivalent to Sindefy, with a dowry provided by the landlady. The aristocratic confidence trickster Sir Petronel Flash, with his imaginary castle, reappears as the Honourable Undecimus Scott with his bogus fortune in shares; the pugnacious attorney Mr Chaffanbrass, is given life by the play's combative Lawyer Bramble; while the adventurers' projected voyage to Virginia is echoed by Alaric Tudor's final voyage to a new world. The most striking example among these minor characters and incidents, however – because it is an incident wholly superfluous to the plot – is the parallel between the Thames shipwreck at Cuckolds' Haven and the collision of Henry Norman's wherry with Chiswick Bridge, which indicates how Trollope could not prevent certain extraneous matter from creeping into the novel unawares.

Trollope's debts to *Eastward Ho!*, with its schematic moral characterization and its contrapuntal plotting, clearly influenced the form of *The Three Clerks*, with its three parallel and interwoven stories, and it is the nature of Trollope's debts to the play that holds the clue to his artistic intention. This goes beyond the superficial prodigal son theme for, as in the play, the truly central issue is how individual ambition may be reconciled with social order. With the growth of a highly complex society in the middle years of the nineteenth century power had begun to shift from the city to the Civil Service, and Trollope knew from his own experience that the ambitions of the intelligent public servant posed the problems of *Eastward Ho!* in a contemporary form. Alaric Tudor's dilemma, which mirrors Quicksilver's, is how to reconcile the paradox of society's simultaneous reverence for material success and for disinterested service. Like Quicksilver and Golding, each clerk nurses a private ambition, which for Charley Tudor is literary fame, for Henry Norman (like Golding) is public respectability, but which for Alaric Tudor represents the Victorian doctrine of individualism in its crudest terms. His growing cynicism is confirmed by his continual exposure in both his professional and domestic life to the double standards of middle-class morality and to its touchstone, Mrs Woodward. She accurately defines competition as the modern disease, but nevertheless strives to secure the three clerks for her daughters and acquiesces in her family's applause for Tudor's 'gumption', regarding him, like they do, as a 'winning horse'. Tudor's obsessive compulsion to compete, not only in the Civil Service but also for the prospective wife of his friend Norman, finally blights his life as, like Quicksilver, he rapidly loses touch with moral reality altogether.

As Trollope argues at length in Chapter XXIX, the modern world is governed by expediency. Convinced of this law by the Mephistophelean Undy Scott, Tudor commences a career of fraud which forms part of a whole series of parallels that includes not only the fiercely ambitious civil servant Sir Gregory Hardlines, but even the Prime Minister who, for the sake of a much needed safe vote, countenances the blurring of public and private interests implicit in Tudor's ambition to enter parliament. The Limehouse and Rotherhithe Bridge affair on which Tudor's fortunes hinge aptly symbolizes this ethos of political corruption, but the novel's central symbol for the fundamental clash between the old morality of social obligation and the new morality of self-help, is the new Civil Service competitive examination. The old patronage system recruited unambitious men like Henry Norman and Fidus Neverbend who help regulate burgeoning industrialization but allow the service to petrify into a system of self-perpetuating oligarchies. But the open examination, which foreshadows the emergence of a meritocracy, also threatens to bring social anarchy by admitting into the public service intelligent and unscrupulous men like Alaric Tudor, who employ their public role solely for private gain.

However, Trollope's satire, like that in *Eastward Ho!*, is two-edged. Like the authors of the play, he recognizes that ambition and energy are inherently admirable and that passivity too often masks moral torpor. Just as the self-righteous preaching of Touchstone and Golding is really little more than a defence of their narrow class concern, the puritanical homilies of Mrs Woodward and Henry Norman also conceal a fundamental self-interest. Their morality is tested at Alaric Tudor's trial where, as in the play, the man of virtue is in a position to restore the moral equilibrium. But in *The Three Clerks* Trollope employs the same situation to present a more tarnished world than that of *Eastward Ho!* in which comic reconciliation and social harmony are achieved. Unlike Golding, Henry Norman's forgiveness of his successful rival really masks a well-judged revenge, while on the public level a society wedded to his double standards requires more than the simple justice meted out in the play: it demands a scapegoat and Tudor is forced to emigrate. Nevertheless, in both the play and the novel it is society that is held responsible for the misdirection of the individual will and, as their parallel of emblematic pattern suggests, the moral worlds of *Eastward Ho!* and *The Three Clerks* include a clearsighted account of the hollowness of social ambition. This is symbolized in the play by the illusory Eastward Castle which Gertrude Touchstone vainly seeks, and in the novel, more realistically, by the citadel of social acceptance which Gertrude Woodward tries to storm – the Chiswick Flower Show. Here in the close contiguity of the inner and outer worlds of London society she has a similar chastening experience of the emptiness of social victory for as Trollope points out: 'Where is the citadel? How is one to know when one has taken it?' (p. 185). She also witnesses the private hypocrisy of respected public figures and watches obsessive ambition progressively destroy her husband's peace of mind and, like the Gertrude of the play, as a result of her disillusioning initiation into marriage and society, Gertrude Woodward's private ambition is modified. But the fundamental problem of her innately competitive will remains. Unlike Quicksilver and Gertrude Touchstone, for whom there is a comic resolution and social reabsorption, for Alaric Tudor and his wife there is no simple answer. As Trollope demonstrates, in Victorian society there is no natural place for truly ambitious spirits and his sympathy at the conclusion of the novel is with its victims who emigrate, as the adventurers in the play desire to do, to a new world where competition with the natural environment offers their energy full scope and social value.

It is evident, I think, that Trollope's debts of character, plotting, situation and moral pattern bestow coherence and vitality on *The Three Clerks*, while the central issue of *Eastward Ho!* is employed to deepen his own sombre criticism of contemporary society, a criticism which is consistent with his later trenchant satire in *The Way We Live Now*. And Trollope again transposes the Jacobean world into Victorian social terms in *Miss Mackenzie*, in which we can see a similar imaginative process at work. Faced with an admitted failure of invention, Trollope began to draw on D'Avenant's *News From Plymouth*, a farcical battle of the sexes dealing with a theme which fascinated him : the subversive power of the independent woman. He makes significant changes of character and milieu, however, for D'Avenant's boisterous port becomes Trollope's puritan spa town Littlebath, and worldly Lady Loveright, who judges her society's moral degeneracy with acerbic wit, is transformed into Trollope's mouthpiece for his own social criticism, the timid, middle-aged middle class spinster, Miss Mackenzie.

Once again Trollope's transposition involves parallels of characterization and details of situation and plotting. D'Avenánt's play concerns three poverty-stricken sea captains who court rich Lady Loveright, her niece Miss Joynture and their affluent landlady the Widow Carrack. The plot of Trollope's novel hinges on the pursuit of the wealthy Miss Mackenzie, who lodges with her niece Susanna at Miss Todd's house in Littlebath, by three impoverished suitors. Trollope is also indebted to D'Avenant's technique of characterization. Like his sea captains, who are 'humour' figures, Trollope's lightly-sketched suitors represent hypocrisy, vulgarity and sheer dullness. While Seawit's intelligence is reflected in the cunning of the curate Maguire, and Cable's vulgarity is echoed by Mr Rubb the tradesman, it is evident that the prosaic integrity of John Ball owes a great deal to the stiff formality and innate honesty of Studious Warwell. Trollope also echoes D'Avenant in the smaller details of his plotting. In both the play and the novel the lady's niece urges the virtues of her dull but honest lover, who is ultimately accepted; and in the end the worldly suitors have to be content, in each case, with what they can get : in *News From Plymouth* Seawit marries Miss Joynture and Cable is trapped by the Widow Carrack, while in *Miss Mackenzie* Maguire is finally caught by Miss Mackenzie's friend, Miss Colza.

In both D'Avenant and Trollope the courtship ritual masks the crude reality of the wealthy single woman's social status as a mere commercial object. As such, Lady Loveright and Miss Mackenzie function as catalysts for the aggressively acquisitive forces in their respective societies, and although the stern morality of Trollope's spa town is far removed from D'Avenant's bustling seaport, in both worlds men thrive on women's social and sexual insecurity. In the cheerfully amoral world of the play this is part of an elaborate game, but in claustrophobic Littlebath it is insidiously concealed by a veneer of piety and here Trollope's severe criticism of the middle class evangelicals who prey remorselessly on the loneliness, frustration and neurotic guilt of middle-aged single women is sharpened by his debts to minor figures in *News From Plymouth*. The garrulous bore Sir Solemn Trifle is employed to flesh out the platitudinous hypocrite the Reverend Mr Stumfold, but a more striking model is the puritan 'humour' character Zeal, whose anti-Papist ranting is echoed by Trollope's curate Maguire.

Both Lady Loveright and Miss Mackenzie are singularly free spirits whose wealth, paradoxically, allows them the necessary freedom to assert the supremacy of moral rather than sexual or social values. They are feared as subversive forces because they courageously pierce the façade of public manners to reveal the shabby falsehoods and covert power that really make society work. In both D'Avenant and Trollope this transformation of vulnerability into moral armour goes hand in hand with the comic motif of the pursuer pursued, by which each potential lover is tested. But while Lady Loveright's social poise allows her to gauge Warwell's devotion by flirting nonchalantly with Seawit, Miss Mackenzie is tormented by her suitors' attentions and agonizes over her choice of John Ball. And in each case tension is added to the moral conflict by the strong undercurrent of sexual rivalry, for Ball bitterly resents the competition of Maguire and Rubb just as Warwell is frantically jealous of Seawit.

In the novel, as in the play, freedom is rooted in acute moral intelligence. For both women marriage must be founded on human equality, and Lady Loveright finally accepts Sir Studious

Warwell only when, for her sake, he has stripped himself of his wealth, books and pleasures; while Miss Mackenzie discards her romantic notions and marries her elderly, impoverished cousin principally because he does not threaten her hard-won independence. Furthermore, D'Avenant and Trollope both recognize that for women freedom must be exercised in the context of social healing. Paradoxically, Lady Loveright and Miss Mackenzie share, together with the need to assert their selfhood, a strong feminine instinct for self-sacrifice, and Lady Loveright's ambition 'to make a man, not take addition from him'[6] is echoed by Miss Mackenzie, who savours the combination of self-sacrifice and social power which her marriage offers. When her husband inherits wealth and a title Miss Mackenzie's match more closely parallels Lady Loveright's aristocratic marriage and her rejection of romantic self-delusion is fully rewarded. Clearly, within the moral framework of *News From Plymouth*, Lady Loveright's decision to love aright renders her match with Sir Studious Warwell a symbolic union of judgement and merit and it is echoed in Trollope's novel by Miss Mackenzie's marriage, which represents the fruitful combination of moral intelligence and human worth. Trollope's debt to D'Avenant thus goes deeper than simply their parallel interest in the power of the independent woman. His close echoing of the play's central plot emphasizes his moral preoccupation with the nature and value of personal freedom and his treatment of this problems gains considerable clarity of focus from his borrowing. However, his significant alterations of character and milieu contribute to the creation of a world which is darker and more threatening than that of the Jacobean dramatist, a recognizably Victorian world in which individual liberty is more difficult to achieve and to sustain.

In *The Three Clerks* Trollope successfully manages to fuse elements of autobiography with his debts to *Eastward Ho!*, but in *Ralph the Heir* the hiatus between the inheritance plot and the election plot marks, I believe, the gulf between his debts to Middleton's *Michaelmas Term* and his reminiscences of his own disillusioning experiences at Beverley in the election of 1868.[7] The plots are only tenuously connected through the relationship of the heir Ralph Newton with his guardian Sir Thomas Underwood who, like Trollope, vainly stands as a candidate in a borough which is subsequently disfranchised. Moreover, the subsidiary plot is in general more vividly compelling than the main plot. This is partly due to the depth of treatment accorded to the character of Sir Thomas Underwood, which was probably based on the complex personality of Trollope's own father, and also to the detail and atmosphere of the election scenes. The inheritance plot which is drawn from Middleton and is altogether different in style, contributes nothing to Trollope's account of contemporary politics because it is concerned with quite separate issues. Here Trollope preserves the basic situation of Middleton's play and in addition the hyperbolic behaviour of his tradesmen, together with the central pattern of character relations, but he also catches the distinctive tone and point of Middleton's satire. Like Middleton, a realist and a moralist, Trollope presents contemporary social tensions with unsentimental clarity. In both the play and the novel the city milieu embraces and symbolizes the central conflict between the impoverished gentry and the rising merchant class and the consequent corruption of rural values by the metropolis. In each case the targets of satiric attack are the avarice of the middle classes and the irresponsible use of capital inherent in a feudal system of inheritance, because as the old country estates pass into the hands of money-lenders and merchants the stability and values of the social order are threatened, while family life is poisoned by the frantic competition for property.

Middleton's city comedy types—the naïve young country heir, the wily city merchant and his rebellious wife and shadowy assistant – all recur in the novel; and there is, moreover, a clear parallel between the way Richard Easy is tricked out of his inheritance by a city woollen-draper and the way in which Ralph Newton and his estate fall into the blackmailing power of his London breeches-maker. Both Quomodo and Neefit, whose social aspirations are frustrated by their middle class background, are driven by an insane desire for social elevation and pin their hopes on their association with the landed gentry. The unspoken barter of sex for lands which motivates Middleton's world becomes explicit in Trollope as Neefit advances Ralph loans in return for a match with his daughter. But each merchant is governed so completely by his monomania that he finally overreaches himself and becomes merely a comic butt. Quomodo feigns death only to discover that his son threatens to ruin the estate and that his wife has made a match with Easy, while more realistically but no less comically, Neefit's impotent rage at his failure to blackmail Ralph is expressed in his smashing of the furniture of the Moonbeam Inn, and his humiliation is compounded by his daughter's subsequent marriage to a cobbler's son. Neefit, as the judge says of Quomodo in *Michaelmas Term*, is his own affliction.

Another important interest for both Middleton and Trollope is the way sexual and social rivalry feed each other and this forms the basis for several parallels of character and situation between the play and the novel. Just as Quomodo's daughter Susan is courted by the well-bred but dissolute gallant Rearage and by the social upstart son of a tooth-drawer Andrew Lethe, Neefit's daughter Polly is pursued by both the rakish heir Ralph Newton and Ontario Moggs, the cobbler's son. Similarly, while Quomodo and his daughter favour Lethe in opposition to his wife's preference for Rearage, Neefit's wife and Polly champion Moggs rather than Newton. Trollope has reversed some of the character relations and simplified this area of the plot, but, as in the play, the motive remains social victory by sexual intrigue and the social status of the suitors is still the key issue.

But essentially Middleton and Trollope are both concerned to examine not only bourgeois greed but the fundamental problem of what weak-minded and corruptible young men are to do with their lives while waiting for their inheritances. Both Richard Easy and Ralph Newton are plainly unfit to inherit their estates, which they tend to regard as useful collateral on which to raise loans, and their predicament points to the moral dangers of idle capital. Easy and Newton are both social parasites, content to batten on the wealthy merchants, and only bitter experience of their victims' wiles and a measure of luck encourage the young gentry to recognize, rather belatedly, their social responsibilities; for just as Easy's redemption commences with the fortuitous trial by which he regains his inheritance, Ralph Newton's reformation hinges on the timely death of his uncle. For the anguished Squire Newton, whose natural son cannot inherit it, the estate represents a tradition of order and social obligation. He is one in the long line of rural gentry portrayed in the past by novelists such as Fielding and Smollett. For these authors the estate could have a forceful symbolic significance as a seat and retreat for the finest values and the security of a passing world. But for the merchants, in both the play and the novel, the acquisition of a country estate offers the only kind of immortality materialism knows. For them it is a commercial possession, but also a symbol of social victory and a means of vengeance on the gentlemen they have served and despised all their lives. In social terms they pose a profound threat to the rural community, but both the play and the novel are also concerned to demonstrate how in private life the struggle for property destroys family relations. For Quomodo's son Sim the inherited estate becomes an irksome obligation, and Ralph's inheritance is the cause of bitter division in the Newton family and the source of the subtle discord between the squire and his son.

In *Ralph the Heir* Trollope's social criticism is given greater force by his adoption of the core of Middleton's plot and by his transposition of the pattern of conflicting forces at work in Jacobean society. But, thematically, while preserving Middleton's comic, satiric treatment of the aspiring merchant class, Trollope has shifted the balance of criticism from this area of society to focus on the underlying problems of capital and the archaic system of inheritance which underpins Middleton's plot. For Trollope, as for Middleton, it divides families, corrupts young heirs, intensifies the competition between city and countryside and increases the stranglehold of the commercial ethic on English social life.

As in the case of *Miss Mackenzie,* in the writing of *Lady Anna,* undertaken on board ship during a voyage to Australia, Trollope's imagination seems to have faltered and once again he turned for assistance to the Jacobean drama. But it is a particularly unusual novel because it is indebted to two different plays, one of which provided Trollope with the basis of his story, while the other helped him over a difficulty of plotting. In *Lady Anna*, unlike those novels previously discussed, Trollope's creative imagination was never really engaged with either the characters or the plots on which he drew. Rather, he deliberately embarked on what was frankly a thesis novel devoted to proving the superiority of education over birth and his borrowing provided him with the technical devices necessary to overcome obstacles to the prosecution of his argument.[8]

Trollope found a solution to the problem of arranging an encounter between a noblewoman and a commoner in the plot of the anonymous pseudo-historical romance *The Weakest Goeth to the Wall*, in which a noble family flee to a Flanders town where a tailor, Barnaby Bunch, protects the mother and daughter from their wicked landlord and squanders all his income in paying their debts. This is the basic situation of *Lady Anna*. Turned out of their home by the evil Earl Lovel, the Countess and her daughter are sheltered by a Keswick tailor, Thomas Thwaite and his son, Daniel. Trollope used Barnaby Bunch, whose humanity shines through his vituperation, as the model for his own rough-tongued tailor, whose staunch moral support of the two noblewomen also involves him in great financial sacrifice. But for a storyteller and a moralist this raised the challenge of arranging a credible situation in which an earl's daughter could marry a tailor 'without glaring fault on her side', as Trollope put it.[9] He found the answer in Ford's *The Fancies Chaste and Noble*,[10] a romance primarily concerned with a ritualistic trial devised in order to prove the virtue of noblewomen, in which Flavia's husband declares in open court that their marriage is null because of his pre-contract. These are exactly the grounds upon which Earl Lovel attempts to nullify his marriage to Josephine Murray and which, as in the play, prove false.[11] This legal plot is essential in gaining the reader's sympathy for the wronged Countess, but more importantly it enables Trollope to allow Anna to grow up in the same household as Daniel Thwaite and to fall in love with him without flouting either social or narrative propriety.

It is against a background of bitter class struggle that

Trollope's own testing of aristocratic virtues finds ironic definition, for the central legal battle over the noblewomen's rights provides a vehicle for his covert examination of human values. The rival claims of birth and education are formulated by juxtaposition. Brought up in a tailor's family, Lady Anna is a working class aristocrat, intensely aware of her ordinariness, while Daniel Thwaite, well educated and possessing an innate nobility, is obviously an aristocrat of the labouring class. But Trollope's closer scrutiny of the claims of birth demonstrates an appalling hiatus between social rank and human worth. Anna's love and her moral education under Thwaite's powerful influence finally prove stronger than mere blood, and her insistence on her pre-contract in the face of fierce psychological pressure contrasts starkly with her father's cynical betrayal of human obligations. And a similar parallel is drawn between the aristocratic Lovel family's readiness to consolidate their social position with the wealth derived from their son's abhorrent marriage with a tailor's lodger (thus circumventing the necessity for a lawsuit over the Lovel inheritance, which they might lose), and the complex monomania of the base-born Countess, who has so completely assimilated the corrupt values of the very family that brought about her ruin that, in spite of her daughter's title and probable independent wealth, she is prepared to kill Thwaite in order to preserve the purity of the family blood.

Trollope felt that society was moving inevitably towards democracy and in *Lady Anna* his sympathy is with the democrats who on the whole place personal values before class allegiance, even when it involves them in self-evidently paradoxical actions. By his quixotic sacrifice, giving succour to the class he hates and which bankrupts and spurns him, Thwaite transcends mere class antagonisms, yet his agreement with the Countess that there can be no union between her class and his affirms the notion of a hierarchy founded on birth. However, his son Daniel, Trollope's spokesman in the novel, is both more humane in his assumption of the simple equality of human worth and more subversive in his conscious assertion of his superior social value. Moreover, by demonstrating in the lives of the radical tailors the traditional aristocratic virtues of concern for moral and social obligations, Trollope satirizes the abstract notion of nobility based in some mystical way on blood, and the overtly symbolic marriage between an aristocrat and a member of the working class which closes the novel deliberately and ironically indicates that there is no innate difference between people. Unfortunately, in *Lady Anna* Trollope's attempt to graft elements of romance plotting onto a realistic study of Victorian social classes weakens both his grasp of character and the effectiveness of his realism. The argument, moreover, is allowed to rest on too hypothetical a case. It avoids the logical consequences of the issues of bitter class struggle it raises and in this instance one is forced to conclude that Trollope's social criticism is severely limited by the very plot material that he adopted from the drama.

The Fixed Period is another novel indebted to the Jacobean drama which fails because of its curious mingling of romance, fantasy and social realism. As Gamaliel Bradford noted, its plot is drawn from *The Old Law* by Massinger, Rowley and Middleton,[12] a play concerned with the testing of the nature and strength of man's fundamental humanity. When Duke Evander revives an ancient law calling for the death of men at the age of eighty and of women at the age of sixty, he makes in effect a searching examination of family loyalties and of the cohesive power of the whole social fabric. The response of the majority of the population to the old law is represented by Simonides, who can scarcely conceal his glee at the prospect of sudden wealth and position when he learns that his father, Creon, is to die. Leonides' son Cleanthes on the other hand, proves the exception. He is so grief-stricken that he even arranges a mock funeral in order to secure his father's escape. Families are everywhere divided by the cruel law, widows are courted in anticipation of their husbands' deaths and social life disintegrates. The play effectively demonstrates how social cohesiveness depends not on love or family loyalty, but on a materialist process of deferred expectations and on the sheer unpredictability of death.

Trollope's interest in the same disillusioning theme is embodied in his parallel plotting in *The Fixed Period*. In the island of Britannula the inhabitants have thrown off British rule and their new Government establishes a series of fresh laws designed to promote social efficiency and general happiness. The 'fixed period' is one of these. Citizens are to be sent to a 'college' at the age of sixty-seven to live in comfort and contemplation for a year while they await euthanasia. The family of Crasweller, the first man to fall victim to this law, crusade against it and they are aided by the President's son Jack Neverbend, who is courting Crasweller's daughter Eva. His rival Grundle however, eager to obtain her father's wealth, lends his support to the law in the Assembly. But unlike the authors of *The Old Law*, Trollope's concern with the human conflict between love and material self-interest is secondary to his satiric attack on utilitarianism, on its inhuman conception of social efficiency and on the tyrannical power of the state. The novel is a bitter satire on social planning, but it also constitutes a political nightmare so horrific that Trollope evades the issue by bringing in the British navy as a *deus ex machina*. The colony is in such consternation at the barbaric law that it gladly capitulates and returns to British rule on the day of Craswaller's incarceration. It has to be said that *The Fixed Period* is a poor novel, hovering uneasily between prophetic fantasy and social satire. With the exception of the President Neverbend, its characters are never convincing and in this case the result of Trollope's indebtedness to the Jacobean drama is one of the strangest novels in the English language.

It is remarkable that Trollope's finest political novel, *The Prime Minister*, is indebted to a Jacobean play, but this is corroborated by the dating of his marginalia. Trollope read Fletcher's *Women Pleased* on 23 March 1874 and began to write *The Prime Minister* on 2 April 1874, just ten days later, while the details of character and plot were still fresh in his mind.[13] He was deeply interested in the theme of Fletcher's play and this, together with elements of plotting, characterization and social comment, is carried over into the novel, informing both its main and subsidiary plots and binding them tightly together.

The villains of the play and the novel, both named Lopez, follow similar occupations: Fletcher's Lopez is a jeweller and usurer while Trollope's Lopez is a financial speculator whose father was a jeweller.[14] Like the Lopez of the play, who marries the wealthy Isabella in order to increase his scope for speculation, Ferdinand Lopez marries Emily to secure finance for his own ventures. To save money Isabella is denied proper food and clothing, while Emily is taken to live at her father's expense in Manchester Square. Isabella's desire for independence is paralleled by Emily's shame at her husband's fraudulent activities which makes a separation seem a moral as well as a personal necessity. Just as in the play Lopez's insane jealousy, fed by Rugio's wooing of his wife, widens the rift between them, when Emily shrinks from her unlovable husband his jealousy is intensified by the competition of her former lover Arthur Fletcher. Each young man fulfils the moral function of testing the woman's virtue and in each case the husband's suspicions are confirmed by his finding wife and lover together. Trollope also preserves the familial nature of the love triangle, for Isabella's lover turns out to be her disguised brother while between Emily's family and Fletcher's there is a long history of close ties.

The second love triangle in *Women Pleased*, which involves Isabella's brother Silvio, Claudio and the Princess Belvidere, is also echoed in *The Prime Minister* by the relation between Lopez, Fletcher and Emily. Like Silvio, Lopez is an interloper whose cardinal sin is social presumption, and Silvio's exclusion from the citadel where Belvidere is guarded by her mother is paralleled by Lopez's banishment from Manchester Square. And in the same way that Silvio uses his aunt Rhodope to gain access to Belvidere, Lopez employs Emily's aunt Roby to outwit Mr Wharton. On the completion of their furtive courtship, Lopez is ostracized by the Whartons. In the same manner the Duchess banishes Silvio, for Belvidere's marriage had been intended to cement a political alliance with the Duke of Siena – just as Emily's proposed match was expected to strengthen the connection with the Fletchers. Trollope is also indebted to Fletcher's plot for further minor details which he subsequently filled out. The violent rivalry between Claudio and Silvio is carried over into the novel when Lopez in a jealous rage pursues

Fletcher with a horsewhip; the supposed death of Claudio probably foreshadows Lopez's suicide, while the wilful Duchess's war with the Duke of Siena, which forms the political background to *Women Pleased*, anticipates the covert rivalry between the Duke and Duchess of Omnium in *The Prime Minister*.

But apart from these closely echoed details of plotting, Trollope is also indebted to the central theme of the play, which links its plots together: women's struggle to achieve 'maistrye' or 'their soveraigne Wills'. Like Fletcher, Trollope is passionately concerned with the woman's acute dilemma of how to reconcile her public roles and private identity and ambition. Women in Trollope's Victorian world are expected to assimilate the contradictions of a society which pays lip-service to ideals such as romantic love, the sacredness of the home and personal liberty, but where in reality they are supposed to function as pawns in the endless struggle for wealth and power. And the central symbol for the novel's thoroughly political and fragmented world, in which even marriage is an uneasy alliance made to preserve class privilege, is the Coalition. Like the Princess Belvidere and Isabella in *Women Pleased*, although they are women of different rank, the Duchess of Omnium and Emily Wharton are alike in rebelling against their coalition marriages. In *Can You Forgive Her?* Trollope is appalled at the way the sheer weight of social will forced the young Glencora to abandon her egalitarian passion for the scapegrace Burgo Fitzgerald for a purely political match with the pedestrian young Palliser; but in *The Prime Minister* he is even more critical of the way the middle classes, like the Whartons and the Fletchers, coyly idealize economic self-interest (I, 163), and he sympathizes with Emily's revolt against the crudely political nature of Victorian family life in marrying the outsider. For both Emily and Glencora however, marriage – the only area for individual fulfilment open to them – becomes a battleground for trenchantly opposed wills. Palliser hampers Glencora's efforts to organize the social aspects of his Government and Emily's dreams of furthering her husband's career are shattered by his secrecy and domestic tyranny. And because their husbands come to symbolize for them society's dehumanizing betrayal of their selfhood, each unconsciously exacts vengeance.

The Victorian confusion of social and sexual roles is partly to blame in both cases. While Glencora has the ambition and the cynical utilitarianism necessary to keep the Coalition alive, Palliser is timid and thin-skinned. Angry that such a man must be 'jury, and judge, and executioner' (I, 364), Glencora endeavours to become the effective Prime Minister herself (I, 320–21), undermining her husband's political confidence until he feels that he is a mere figurehead (I, 195). In doing so she is gratifying a desire for a sexual as well as a social revenge on the husband she cannot truly love. Choosing a time when her husband's judgement is clouded, she secretly champions the mysterious interloper Lopez (who reminds her of Burgo Fitzgerald) in the Silverbridge election, and so contributes to the gradual collapse of the Government. Emily Wharton's militant feminism, her refusal to submit to her family's choice of either life-defeating virginity or a marriage 'within the pale' (I, 176) has a sexual motivation too. Her lover, Arthur Fletcher, treats her as his 'holy of holies' (I, 187) when she frankly wants to be 'mastered' by Lopez (I, 452). But, horrified by the crude realities of Victorian life which Lopez represents, she later retreats behind her family's tribal judgement of him as an abhorred foreigner. Trollope's treatment of Lopez becomes more sympathetic and his criticism of Emily more stringent as the schizoid quality of her nature emerges. Overtly a model Victorian wife patiently enduring her boorish husband, like Isabella and Belvidere in *Women Pleased* and like the Duchess of Omnium, she is working assiduously for her own triumph, coolly playing on his male vulnerability, his financial dependence, his social and sexual insecurity, until her passive assertion of blind will forces him into excesses, public humiliation and suicide. Characteristically, Emily responds to his death with a further piece of self-deception. Her abject penitence for the 'persistency of [her] perverse self-will' (II, 397) refers, she tells herself, to her social rebellion; but it more truthfully and accurately describes the final unrepentant triumph of her will in marrying Arthur Fletcher.

Like Fletcher in *Women Pleased*, Trollope is fiercely critical of a society that classes its women as outsiders and ignores their legitimate claims to selfhood expressed in terms of social value. One of the dominant ironies of the novel is that while it is the women who possess will and energy, they are made subject to the crushing weight of social convention invoked by weak men like Palliser, Wharton and Fletcher. Trollope portrays Victorian society as totally enervated, desperately in need of people of vision and drive, and inevitably, he suggests, women of powerful will may become a frustrated and subversively destructive force. As in the play, this theme is closely woven into the structure of the novel, binding together its subsidiary plots and giving it both vigour and formal precision. *The Prime Minister* offers the fullest example of Trollope's debts to a play thoroughly permeating a novel from the larger elements of character and structure down to the smaller details of plotting, and I believe this is mainly due to the fact that *Women Pleased* was still fresh in his memory, informing his imagination as he wrote.

Trollope's debt to the Jacobean drama is more extensive than scholars have supposed; and his borrowing, which spans his entire career as a novelist, contributes to both his successes and his comparative failures. Plainly, *Ralph the Heir*, *Lady Anna* and *The Fixed Period* suffer from Trollope's inability to assimilate fully his various debts, but *Miss Mackenzie* on the other hand, is redeemed from conventionality by his adoption of D'Avenant's spirited comedy. Because of its debt to *Eastward Ho! The Three Clerks* is developed with a surer sense of form and artistic purpose than critics have recognized, and similarly *The Prime Minister* gains greater moral penetration and clarity of design from Trollope's borrowing from Fletcher. These debts are equally important in shedding further light on the nature and workings of Trollope's imagination. Essentially, it is a synthesizing imagination, which utilizes traditional forms and ideas by transposing them into Victorian social terms. However, Trollope clearly felt that his world was altogether more complex, darker and more bewildering than that offered by the comedies and romances on which he drew. He transforms them into sombre novels, possessing a bleaker and a more trenchantly satirical social criticism. And this treatment of his adoption of characters, plots, themes, situations and incidents from the Jacobean drama suggests, in my view, that the innate bias of Trollope's mind is more radical than critics have believed.

Scene and Form

The power of Trollope's form is a striking but still relatively disregarded aspect of his art. This is partly due to his undeserved reputation as a mechanical craftsman, but it is also because the expansive nature of his novels resists post-Jamesian critical notions. Against James's view of mid-Victorian novels as 'baggy monsters' needs to be set the judgement of W.P. Ker, who noted Trollope's affinity with the *Comédie Humaine* but considers him the greater artist because '[h]e is a dramatist, and Balzac is not'.[15] In the dramatic novel, as in the drama, the individual scene is a subject in its own right and as the smallest unit of the action it is an important source of the reader's insight into the meaning of the novel. Trollope has an instinctive sense of its form and function, but his achievements in the use of scene are also rooted in his careful study of the early drama. His marginalia frequently insist that scenes must possess dramatic fullness and aesthetic completeness,[16] and in an article on Henry Taylor he argues that it is by means of its scenes that drama 'forces the reader to identify himself . . . with the images and creations of the author'.[17]

Trollope's close interest in the relation between the individual scene and the ampler form of the novel emerges in his remarks on the function of the scene together with a scenario in an article for *Good Words*:

. . . rules as to construction have probably been long known to [the novelist]. . . . They have come to him from much observation, from the writings of others, from that which we call study, – in which imagination has but little immediate concern. It is the fitting of the rules to the characters which he has created, the filling in with living touches and true colours those daubs and blotches on his canvas which have been easily scribbled with a rough hand, that the true work consists.[18]

These 'rules as to construction' constitute the basis of the scenarios to be found among Trollope's work sheets. But the vitality of character so vividly presented in his novels resides in the dramatic scene, and its creation is the 'true work' which demands imaginative power :

The first coarse outlines of his story [the novelist] has found to be a matter almost indifferent to him. It is with these little plotlings that he has to contend . . . Every little scene must be arranged so that, – if it may be possible, – the proper words may be spoken and the fitting effect produced.[19]

This shaping process is not determined by any vague pictorial aesthetic, although Millais found Trollope's novels a pleasure to illustrate. It is much more than an intense visualization of the action for it involves a careful structuring of these 'little plots' in which 'incident or the character was moulded and brought into shape'.[20] An important aspect of Trollope's solution to the problem of form in the novel is his employment of scene in conjunction with a scenario composed of points of development in plotting and characterization, which allows flexibility in planning and yet achieves precision and point in execution. His artistic gains lie in his use of closely related techniques which are translated from the dramatic to the fictional form.

G. G. Sedgewick's perception that the drama is an ironic convention is also true of the dramatic novel.[21] In its scenes the reader looks from the real world into a world of illusion, obtaining an elevated view of it and observing it with a mixture of detachment and sympathy. Irony is the essential tool of both the dramatist and the dramatic novelist for in the scene what strikes the reader most is not the portrayal of inward character but the dynamic relation between characters in conflict. The scene is an oblique means of communication with the reader because the author's voice comes through a seemingly objective presentation. Its central irony resides in the reader seeing his own wisdom confirmed by events. In the well-known confrontation between Mr Crawley and the Bishop of Barchester in *The Last Chronicle of Barset* this kind of irony is potent on several levels. In the Bishop's presence the perpetual curate of Hogglestock assumes a studied meekness which the reader knows to be the political strategy of a proud, forceful man and despite his initial blandness, the reader is aware that the Bishop is not only timid but impotent in the matter of Mr Crawley's preaching from his own pulpit. Nor is Mrs Proudie's submissiveness natural, but is the result of a prior quarrel with her husband over the legality of the Bishop's 'inhibition'. There is thus an opening irony of manners which requires a moderation of pace, for their self-control depends on the rigorous suppression of emotion.

The ironic movement of the scene, the recognition of the curate's power, is given impetus by his prior insight into the Bishop's misery. His wry smile of understanding goads Mrs Proudie to the rudeness which invokes Mr Crawley's magisterial rebuke: ' "Peace, woman . . . The distaff were more fitting for you" ' (I, 192) that has the Bishop on his feet. There is a high irony in the down-at-heel curate lecturing the Bishop and his wife, but it is an irony compounded of recognition and reversal of fortune as Mr Crawley ignores the palatial trappings they had relied on to subdue him and forces instead a reluctant acknowledgement of his intellectual and political strength. Instead of the Proudies sacrificing the obscure man in their political battle with the Framley set, he uses them to gain a temporary but immensely satisfying victory over the forces that are crushing him. As one of the older order of clergy in Barsetshire, Mr Crawley presents in its most potent form the challenge of the ascetic life of priestly authority, but blinded by their limited political aims the Bishop and his wife fail to recognize the curate's spiritual integrity and feel only the humiliation of their defeat. For the reader there is not only the primitive identification with the underdog in his fight against institutional oppression, but the perception of the ironic emergence of the true nature of revolution within the Church.

In Trollope the ironic nature of the dramatic scene works in conjunction with dialogue as the revealing medium of the details and motives of a situation. In *Orley Farm* the scene of debate

at the Bull Inn, Leeds, between the Hamworth attorney Dockwrath and the commercial traveller Moulder, demonstrates
Trollope's fine dramatic control. Here dialogue, characters and
theme are synthesized as conflicting parties embody contrasted
ideas. The generation of the action focuses the reader's attention
on the dialogue itself, which produces a strong dialectical force
propelling the scene's emotion and action. The debate centres
on Dockwrath's refusal to abide by the unwritten rules concern-
ing the use of the commercial room of the hotel where he has
taken up residence, which Moulder attempts to enforce. The
irony lies in the obese, bullying traveller's assumption of the role
of prosecuting counsel, while the gaunt young lawyer staunchly
defends his commercial interests, and the commercial men stay-
ing at the hotel form the jury. The setting of the 'trial', the commercial room, completes the visual irony, and the legal form of
the argument with its dialectical pattern, lends an ironic richness to the dialogue. Moulder's case, that because Dockwrath
is not a commercial man he is not entitled to the privileges of
the room, is defended by the attorney on the grounds that he is
a commercial lawyer, and the ironies of this statement illumine
the whole scene. In one sense Dockwrath is truly a commercial
man for he runs a lodging house in Hamworth, but Moulder,
aware only of the lawyer's intention to deceive, takes the assertion as a lie. As the reader knows, however, Dockwrath has just
completed an errand to Groby Park to sell legal information
and thus in an invidious way he has indeed become commercial.
Moreover, he consciously associates himself with the business
ethic by using their room and he matches the arrogance of the
commercial men in the legalistic battle in which they are engaged by invoking the law to defeat the obvious justice of
Moulder's claim. The dialogue of the scene thus cooperates
with its ironic structure to bring about a balanced development
of the action, elaborating and intensifying its impressions and
giving direction to the reader's moral interest. Its synthesis is
the uneasy compromise as the travellers leave the room to
Dockwrath, both sides claiming victory. But the failure in communication only masks the corrupting association of self-interest

as Trollope obliquely suggests the degrading collaboration of the law with commerce and its capacity to pervert justice.

The dramatic scene in the novel is a fairly limited area of time and its significant impact depends upon the reader's sense of closure and completion. This effect demands a formal rhythm and tempo which is traced in the smaller climaxes that help to shape its meaning. For instance, in the scene in which Mr Crawley visits the Bishop's palace this development depends initially on the opening irony of manners which the reader has to recognize and which is revealed by the characters' manoeuvring for dominance. The rhythmic pattern of the whole interview is carefully composed as the Bishop's blandness is shaken first by the curate's ready acquiescence and then by his wife's interruption. The minor crisis is marked by silence, the bewildered shaking of the Bishop's head and Mr Crawley's smile of sympathy. After the silence, which allows the reader a fraction of time to assimilate what he has 'seen', the tempo rises again as Mrs Proudie stridently responds to this challenge; and the changed pattern of speech conventions, as Mr Crawley's careful argument begins to overwhelm the Bishop and as Mrs Proudie's interjections gather venom, is a measure of the altered balance of power which leads naturally to the climax. As the implacable confrontation which underlay the opening polite-ness is revealed in the curate's open rebuke, they jump to their feet in response to the attack and the curate marches out.

The rhythm of this scene is Trollope's basic means of organiz-ing the reader's understanding of the emerging irony and it is instructive to measure its success against the same scene in his subsequent play, *Did He Steal It?*. Much of its point is lost by making Mr Crawley a schoolmaster and Dr Proudie a local magistrate. But Trollope also destroys the whole structure of the encounter. The ironic effect of the preliminary tactics is missing, for they both sit. The dramatic rhythm is further nullified because in the play Mr Crawley is defensive from the outset and his 'I am . . . guiltless before the law' is much less dramatic than in the novel where he makes his subtle early challenge to the Bishop over its interpretation. Similarly, Mrs Goshawk's antagonism emerges too early. Her 'I am glad you

obeyed our summons' and 'Yes, sir; and Mr Goshawk is express-
ing his opinion . . .' are lines which are given in the novel to
the Bishop. Her vigorous attack and Mr Crawley's early capitulation thus prevent any possibility of dramatic growth. Except
for minor alterations, the dialogue is identical with the novel,
but the interview is flat and undramatic. Mrs Goshawk bears
all the burden of the conversation and her husband is little
more than a mild echo, so that the reader misses her usurping
interruptions and the comic dislocation that allows the curate
to take the initiative. His fine closing lines are retained but they
miss their biblical irony and in fact lose their impact altogether
because Mr Crawley has already addressed them to his wife.
In the play they merely mark the close of a vulgar squabble,
and their function as exit lines is denied by the need for dramatic compression which forces Trollope to continue a discussion
at the end of the scene between Mr Crawley and Grace about
Mrs Goshawk's son Captain Oakley. This conflation prevents
Trollope from rescuing any vestige of dramatic significance from
the scene. It is a strange paradox that scenes in Trollope's novels
are more truly dramatic than in his two plays, but he needed
the imaginative scope of the scenario to keep true scale in his
scenic structure and detail.

Within the limited area of time that the scene constitutes the
dramatic writer's sense of space is also important in creating its
rhythm and Trollope excels in presenting sharply detailed and
composed groups set in a potentially dramatic relation to each
other. The dramatic scene is often a microcosm of the conflicting
human forces in the novel and in *Barchester Towers* this is true
of Mrs Proudie's reception. Scale is kept by Trollope's careful
use of a clear social perspective. It is the first confrontation of
the political forces of the diocese after Mr Slope's divisive
sermon and is a gesture made to cement its factions. Its function
of papering over the cracks is imaged in Mrs Proudie's efforts to
hide the dowdy appearance of her cheap furnishings. Gesture
and grouping chart the currents of the emotional action as some
kind of attack is expected from the Grantly set. But it comes
from an entirely unexpected source because, of all people, the
Bohemian Stanhopes share an instinctive complicity to subvert

Mrs Proudie's political efforts. The irony is carefully prepared as the guests arrive; as their father hides in a corner of the crowded reception room; as Madeline makes arrangements for the positioning of her sofa; and scale is kept as the Bishop becomes entangled first with the fascinating 'Madame Neroni' and then with her brother Bertie.

The central movement of the scene, the comic attack on Mrs Proudie's hypocrisy, is more than finely-judged farce. The sudden exposure of the underproppings of her finery is the perfect dramatic image for her inherent vulgarity, given point by her furious 'Unhand it, sir!' (I, 97) in response to Bertie's proffered assistance. It is as though the runaway sofa has obeyed the collective will of the assembly in order to prick her arrogance as she achieves her aim of capturing attention, but only as a figure of fun. The irony of Mrs Proudie's comic reversal prompts the reader's recognition of her dehumanizing moral stupidity. However, there is also a muted effect of sympathy as the uneasy equilibrium of the reception is disrupted to reassert the schism in the diocese between those who rejoice at her exposure and those who do not. While the reader partly identifies with the helpless victim at the centre of the room, he also sympathizes with the figures clustered in the background as their excitement at the mishap grows out of their awareness of its social scope and meaning.

Trollope's gift for conferring space and movement on his characters is due to the extra dimension which drama allows. This depends to a large extent on his economical use of settings which gain emblematic significance for character through the accumulation of detail. Trollope makes the reader aware of the emotional background of a scene while focusing on the foreground action. In *The Claverings*, for instance, the moral atmosphere of Clavering Park is given in the scene of Sir Hugh's homecoming after the death of his infant son. A fearful repressive moral area is suggested as the night air strikes his wife shivering at the top of the staircase, and she feels his chill egoism in the way he meticulously removes his street clothes in the hallway before coming up to greet her. The breath of cold air, the delay, the hand nervously grasping the banister rail are all given from Hermione's point of view and they summarize the atmosphere of indifference and blind will in which she is trapped.

Trollope's dramatic realism also depends to an important extent on the characteristically fine balance he achieves between character and setting. Places affect actions. As Lily Dale knows, the gardener in the greenhouse is a different person from the gardener in the house. People are aware of the value and meaning of place and this is turned to comic effect in Mrs Proudie's reception and the curate's visit to the palace, as character adroitly steps outside its conventional limitations. But in Trollope's works characters usually reflect their surroundings although they are not determined by them, and setting thus possesses a quiet relevance to human action. The cold secretiveness of Sir Hugh Clavering is imaged in his square stone house, half-shuttered against intruding eyes, while Ullathorne Court is described in more and warmer detail because it is full of the life and passion of the Thornes for the old ways. The sham of the rich Broughtons is reflected in their Bayswater residence, 'not made of stone yet looking very stony' (*The Last Chronicle of Barset*, I, 244); but the ultimate withdrawal from life is presented in the insane Mr Kennedy whose house, a mere set of 'Ionic columns' through which the visitor passes to the 'broad stone terrace before the door' (*Phineas Finn*, I, 124) symbolizes his emptiness.

Trollope occasionally employs setting to focus objectively the inward mind of a character in a state of crisis and this is deftly achieved in *The Last Chronicle of Barset* when Mrs Dobbs Broughton hears of her husband's suicide: 'Everything was changed with her, – and was changed in such a way that she could make no guess as to her future mode of life. She was suddenly a widow, a pauper, and utterly desolate, – while the only person in the whole world that she really liked was standing close to her. But in the midst of it all she counted the windows of the house opposite' (II, 260). While it realistically evokes her state of shock, setting here also suggests her emotional void and her lack of moral perception. Even the sophisticated Dalrymple is aghast at the vacuum which is revealed and in this scene the

London world is shown to be very different from that of Barsetshire, where the parallel death of Mr Harding is a source of moral insight and self-evaluation.

In Trollope's comedy, too, setting has complete dramatic relevance. It is not the rhetorical scene-setting of Dickens, but there is nevertheless a covert and joyful collaboration between setting and character in *Barchester Towers* after the Archdeacon's first introduction to the new bishop, his wife and his chaplain, when Mr Harding mildly exclaims that he will not find it possible to like Mr Slope:

'Like him!' roared the archdeacon, standing still for a moment to give more force to his voice; 'like him!' All the ravens of the close cawed their assent. The old bells of the tower, in chiming the hour, echoed the words; and the swallows flying out from their nests mutely expressed a similar opinion. Like Mr Slope! Why no, it was not very probable that any Barchester-bred living thing should like Mr Slope! 'Nor Mrs Proudie either,' said Mr Harding.

The archdeacon hereupon forgot himself. I will not follow his example, nor shock my readers by transcribing the term in which he expressed his feeling as to the lady who had been named. The ravens and the last lingering notes of the clock bells were less scrupulous, and repeated in corresponding echoes the very improper exclamation. (1, 42).

In Chapter XIX 'Barchester by Moonlight' Trollope achieves a counterpoint of mood by a dramatic and functional use of the time of day. Eleanor Bold, Mr Slope and the Stanhopes, taking a walk on a summer night, discover that the old city, so mundane and so busy with the petty cares of its inhabitants by day, has undergone a breathtaking transformation, and its beauty stills their quarrelsome natures. The scene creates a temporary emblem of harmony which suggests the possibility of beauty and order in a world of disequilibrium and ferment. It heightens by contrast the ensuing scenes of battle in the diocese, for although Barchester people have the moral capacity to appreciate such rare moments of equipoise, they are ironically incapable of achieving them in the social world.

Thus in a fundamental way Trollope's use of the dramatic scene to articulate the meaning of the novel depends on his careful planning of the scenario.[22] There is, for example, an apparently minor scene which occurs at the physical and moral centre of *The Way We Live Now* in which Father Barham, the Roman Catholic priest from Suffolk, pays his audacious visit to the great commercial man, Melmotte. The priest's background has been meticulously drawn. He is an obscure figure on the very fringe of English society, while Melmotte is its centre and catalyst; and while Barham is an English gentleman, Melmotte is a foreign Jew. This quiet but deliberate contrast serves to draw attention to their moral likeness. Melmotte's devotion to credit, unsupported by any underlying fiscal reality, is essentially similar to Barham's faith in the dogma of his Church, for credit is divorced from capital in the same way that dogma has become estranged from faith. The priest's employment of any means to secure converts is not unlike Melmotte's weird capitalism. The priest will use Melmotte's money to buttress his Church just as the entrepreneur is manipulating religious groups to gain support for his bid to enter parliament and extend his capacity for credit. Further, each loves the exercise of power for its own sake and each comes to believe in his own infallibility. However, Barham is a religious fanatic in an age in which wealth has become the new faith. As Trollope points out: '[i]t seemed that there was but one virtue in the world, commercial enterprise, – and that Melmotte was its prophet' (I, 411). Everyone is involved in the new world and the implication of the Church in this scene indicates the scope of the corrupting association.

The emblematic and satirical value of the scene, however, lies in its ironic structure which produces a careful reversal of the reader's expectations. Instead of a lecture by the Victorian clergyman to the arrogant rich man, the priest himself comes on a speculative enterprise and Melmotte's 'Who the d[evil] are you?' (II, 55) has a mordant irony. It is also potentially a scene of moral recognition, but although Barham is given the rare opportunity of catching Melmotte off his guard he is too bigoted to perceive the depths of his deceit. In an earlier scene the Bishop of Elmham has been discussing with Barham, in a smug, pseudo-religious way, Christ's coming to the Romans. Here the priest is face to face with the Antichrist of the modern world but, ironically, in spite of all the evidence, Barham falls prey to the process of fantasy creation which sustains Melmotte's power and by an exercise of specious casuistry goes away believing the brutish man to be a good Catholic. Surprisingly, it is a process that traps Melmotte as well. As Trollope comments at the close of the scene, these gaudy and grandiose preparations for the Emperor of China's dinner demonstrate that 'the most remarkable circumstance in the career of this remarkable man was the fact that he came almost to believe in himself' (II, 57).

This scene is also a place where the reader's vision rests while there is a subterranean movement of the action. There is a concealed structural irony, for the scene in fact represents the apex of the two men's careers. It is Barham's most audacious venture before he retires to the obscurity of Suffolk, and Melmotte is soon to discover that the tide of rumour has turned against him and his wheel of fortune has started its downward turn. But the main impact of the scene is as a symbol of the world of the novel as a whole. The mediation of the needy aristocracy between the entrepreneur and the priest, the angry incoherence of the conversation, the murky quality of human intercourse encompassed by the tinsel trappings of unfettered materialism make it a potent symbol for Trollope's modern hell.

In the dramatic novel then, scenes have a relevance to the form of the novel as a whole. They present clues to its meaning; for the reader's search for significance in a Trollope novel must always be in the abstract, and yet at the same time dramatic, conflict of ideas and modes of action. This essentially spatial pattern, however, is rooted in the temporal development of the novel. At the beginning the reader wishes to know why the conflict of wills is necessary and the function of the opening scene is to create the dramatic environment which contains it. In *Barchester Towers* the comic disequilibrium in society is focused in the incongruity between the ideal of the Church and its reality as a merely temporal institution. Like the battle between the old and the new, this fundamental split is already present as Archdeacon Grantly watches at the bedside of his dying father, torn between his desire for a bishopric and his love for the gentle old man. This inner conflict is evoked emblematically by the entry of Mr Harding, who stands at the kneeling man's shoulder, the embodiment of his conscience, as Grantly repents of his naked ambition. Although the scene is muted, the rare inside view of Grantly that we are given deftly serves to set apart the elegaic mood of the old world from the comic world of the new bishop, a world of power struggles rather than inner moral strivings. What is more, the conflict overlaps with Trollope's political world from the start; there is an emblematic aptness in Grantly's use of the new-fangled telegraph to wire his urgent message to London and in the demise of the old ministry which makes an ironic parallel with his father's death. But the full relevance of this finely-judged opening scene is only apparent at the conclusion of the novel when the unworldly Mr Harding defeats the divisive tactics of the Archdeacon by renouncing the deanery in favour of Arabin in order to maintain the necessary delicate balance of diocesan power. Just as the anarchic Madeline Stanhope's uncharacteristic efforts at reconciliation succeed on the social level, so in the political sphere Mr Harding demonstrates surprising insight and force as he re-establishes equilibrium in the clerical world. Grantly's self-regarding desire for power, which his old friend thought unseemly, is thus nullified as the emblematic significance of the opening scene is translated into fact.

One important aspect of Trollope's realism is his ability to employ dramatic structural techniques in the novel so that scenes transcend the individual novel and span the years, making a larger temporal pattern. Trollope's recognition of the function of Mr Harding in Dr Grantly's inner life at the beginning of *Barchester Towers* allows his death, the serenity of which reminds Grantly of his father's saintliness, to make the parallel quietly emphatic. This scene provides the Archdeacon with an astonishing moment of understanding of the deeper nature of his relation with his father-in-law. It prompts him to make the alien judgement that the old man he had often scorned had 'all the spirit of a hero' (*The Last Chronicle of Barset*, II, 421), and this revelation that the meek old man has been a father-figure to the bullying, worldly cleric and the source of the conscience that moderated his actions is a profound psycho-logical and moral insight which provides the reader with the shock of recognition that realism demands. Yet Trollope had prepared for it in the quiet opening scene of *Barchester Towers*.

This kind of temporal placing and ironic balance is apparent in Mr Crawley's interview with the Bishop. The irony of his infuriating smile gathers increased significance in the life of Mrs Proudie as it drives her to unparalleled interference in Church matters when she humiliates her husband in front of the powerful Dr Tempest, so undermining his authority in the diocese that he wishes her dead. The collapse of her marriage and the removal of the comic mask has an ironic point for it reveals that in truth it was she who was dependent on her husband. When he sinks into apathy and gloom, she dies. This recognition, which accompanies her reversal of fortune, is a source of moral discovery and it enforces the sense of contra-diction between appearance and reality, which is shown to be an integral and surprising part of the reality of human life. And it sends the reader searching back over the cumulative growth of her monomania which was there unheeded in her meeting with the Archdeacon at the beginning of *Barchester Towers*. In retro-spect the battle with the rebellious curate emerges as something different from what the reader was led to believe. It presented an opportunity for moral recognition and growth that was not grasped. Not only that, but the scene of their encounter was in fact an ironic turning-point in their lives; for as Mr Crawley's smile fed her anger and set her on a destructive path it also marked a change in the psychological health of the curate and foreshadowed his ultimate vindication.

Such scenes are part of the evolution of cause and effect in the lives of the characters and the most important of them are necessary in a fundamental sense, for they are part of the drama-tic rhythm of the novel. They mark a major point in the narrative where the characters experience a break between motives and effects and have to adjust to altered circumstances. They are important moments of moral recognition and the first and most prominently placed is that in which the first cycle of the action culminates and which checks its momentum. Most obviously this is true of the scene of Lady Mason's abrupt and unexpected confession to Sir Peregrine Orme that she forged her husband's will and is in truth guilty of the crime for which she is being tried. It is one of the central dramatic scenes in *Orley Farm*, tense with the emotions of love and shock, of recognition and reversal, and it results in each of the lovers having to re-evaluate their future relation. The rest of the action develops out of the changed balance of forces. And these pivotal scenes are carefully prepared for. In *The Last Chronicle of Barset*, for instance, the clash between the palace and Mr Crawley is antici-pated in the opening discussion by the Walker family which outlines for us the scope of the conflict; by Mrs Proudie's mind-less opposition to the Framley set; by Mr Crawley's trenchant rejection of Mr Thumble's message and by the joyful and faintly silly martyrdom of his long walk to Barchester. The sequence of cause and effect is broken by the Proudies' recognition of the difference between the probabilities as they estimated them – that Mr Crawley would be cowed and submissive at the palace – and the altered necessities that lie ahead of them as this assumption proves totally false.

The conclusions of Trollope's novels frequently embody the conventional recognition scenes of the drama. They are often a complex set of scenes which complete character and structure and which possess unusual moral significance. They show how the forces that shaped the conflict also give meaning to its con-clusion, for in the dramatic novel the end is implied in the beginning. In *The Claverings*, for instance, the quietly emblema-tic final scene is one which completes the major ironic reversal in the novel as the super-jilt, Lady Ongar, who has failed to regain Harry Clavering's love, talks to his future wife, the prudent Florence Burton, in the same grounds of Clavering Park where she had refused him in the opening scene in favour of wealth and position. She recalls her prophecy that she would return to Clavering only when Harry is married, and observes that it is now being fulfilled. But the concealed irony, which even in the bitterness of self-mockery she is too generous to reveal to the naïve Florence, is that the prudence which took Harry away from her was not the result of his deepest instinctive choice, but the product of social forces he was not strong enough to withstand. Seen in these terms, the marriage which ends the novel is not a conventional gesture of hope for the future but is, instead, inconclusive and bitterly ironic.

Trollope's scenic method of presenting character and developing action is varied. Not all scenes are crises. In most of Trollope's vast, panoramic novels there are a number of quiet domestic scenes with a less immediate commitment to plot. These serve to familiarize the reader with character before it is set in action, like the Walkers' conversation about Mr Crawley at the beginning of *The Last Chronicle of Barset;* or to give added depth to the novel's perspective by suggesting the unremittingly normal background of daily life, like the Noningsby scenes in *Orley Farm* or, as in *The Bertrams*, those quiet domestic scenes which obscure private tragedy. And sometimes they capture the moral atmosphere of a social group like the Burtons in *The Claverings*, whose class attitudes have a crucial function in the narrative. But another kind of scene which possesses a convincing reality for the reader is that in which the action is hidden beneath an exterior surface on which nothing very much appears to be happening. For instance, in *The Eustace Diamonds* Lucinda Roanoke's love of hunting at first seems no more than an expression of a healthy athleticism and sociability. However, the scene in which she meets Sir Griffin Tewett in the hunting field is fraught with the concealed tensions of covert manoeuvring as her aunt, Mrs Carbuncle, seeks to marry her to the highest bidder. The odious Sir Griffin is attracted by Lucinda's physical power and her curious hatred of sexuality, and the hunter swiftly becomes the pursued. The scene of the hunt thus gains a complex emblematic significance for the perverted sexuality of the society of *The Eustace Diamonds* and it turns Lucinda Roanoke's life in the direction of personal tragedy.

Trollope's realism is most effective in those scenes devoted to the portrayals of ordinary family life like the conversation between the Duke of Omnium and his sons at the breakfast table in *The Duke's Children*. But the character of the Duke himself is best revealed in *The Prime Minister* in one of those odd little scenes which are so often related to plot and theme in an unob-trusive way when, in the middle of the great political entertain-ment at Gatherum, the Prime Minister disappears for a walk in the grounds with old Lady Rosina De Courcy. Their discussion of the merits of cork soles emphasizes his absorption in mun-dane matters like decimal coinage. But this scene has wider implications, for the Duke is sensitively aware of the vulgarity of the party from which he has temporarily escaped and recog-nizes his conspicuous lack of the tact and *bonhomie* necessary to the leader of a Coalition Government. More disturbing for him is the fact that his wife, in organizing these gatherings, is beginning to dominate not only the uneasy coalition of their marriage but (he fears) the Government as well, for, witty and gregarious, she is the truly political creature of the two. His walk with Lady Rosina is thus not simply an expression of the greater ease that he feels in the company of the old Whig aris-tocracy, nor merely an escape from the tedious duty of seeing to his guests; but his absence from the huge party on such a frivolous pretext offers a covert challenge to his wife's efforts and to the principle of coalition itself in both private and public life. As the novel reveals, it is the Prime Minister who helps to sabotage the Government, and at the very time when, ironically, he was becoming subtly enamoured of power.

In his complex employment of the dramatic scene then, Trollope's aesthetic sense consistently serves his realism. This aspect of his art is so well concealed that it has been overlooked, but in the major novels his scenes are all thematically placed and related and they make an unremitting contribution to his moral vision. Trollope's art depends to a large extent on his judicious use of scene and scenario, but in a real sense it derives from the conviction that what he dramatized really was dramatic.

III
THE FORM OF
THE STORY

The Open Form: *The Last Chronicle of Barset*

THE sheer scope and complexity of a panoramic novel like *The Last Chronicle of Barset*, which Trollope believed was his best work, are basically an expression of his need to give some kind of articulation to the growth and crowdedness of his world. For this reason Jerome Thale, for instance, argues that plot is not important as an element in the structure of this novel and he stresses instead the spatial quality of its design. He reminds us that Trollope himself regarded plot as 'the most insignificant part of a tale' and as merely the 'vehicle' for the narrative.[1] Jerome Thale therefore views the form of *The Last Chronicle of Barset*, with its gradual accumulation of situations and events in spatial patterns, as analogous to painting or music.[2] However, in my view traditional plotting does have an essential function in Trollope's design of the novel and a closer analogy to the multiple plotting in *The Last Chronicle of Barset*, with its parallels and contrasts of character and situation, juxtapositions and criss-crossing of lives and worlds, is not painting or music, but the Jacobean drama.

Ruth apRoberts has argued cogently that as a moralist, Trollope's preferred form, the 'shaping principle' of his fiction as she terms it, is the neatly circumscribed moral situation of novels like *The Warden*.[3] As I shall argue later in this chapter, there is some truth in this view, but we should remember that like his close friend George Eliot Trollope was a diligent observer of the larger world of English society and in his best fiction acute personal moral dilemmas are worked out in an organic relation to the wider circles of social life that encompass them. In *The Last Chronicle of Barset* he succeeds brilliantly in amplifying this principle into an appropriate form for a panoramic study of English social life for as its title implies, the novel is not simply the story of Mr Crawley and the missing cheque, but is a sustained moral exploration of a whole contemporary world: the story of society at a point of change. And in order to achieve this Trollope employed traditional techniques of dramatic plotting.

Of course the term 'plot' has long been a stumbling block in Trollope criticism, partly because Trollope himself employs it in two different senses in his *Autobiography*. When he speaks of plot as the 'vehicle' for the story it is clear from the context of his discussion of Wilkie Collins's sensational novels that he means the external mechanics of the narrative design. However, elsewhere in the *Autobiography* Trollope minimizes the care he expends on the narrative; he stresses instead his serious artistic attention to the function of subsidiary plots and makes it clear that his solution to the form of the story lay in his examination of the technique of multiple plotting:

Though [the novelist's] story should be all one, yet it may have many parts. Though the plot itself may require but few characters, it may be so enlarged as to find its full development in many. There may be subsidiary plots, which shall all tend to the elucidation of the main story, and which will take their places as part of one and the same work . . .'[4]

Thus plot, in its traditional sense, is fundamental to the form of the story in *The Last Chronicle of Barset*. The techniques associated with multiple plotting provide a dynamic means of combining the thematic concentration of the moral fable with a comprehensive study of a whole world. The subsidiary plots form compositional centres in the novel, each embodying a different aspect of its dominant theme. The story is thus an integrating power, bringing all the plots and characters into significant relation, and it is finally revealed as a static moral design as well as an organic creation. In *The Last Chronicle of*

Barset there are a number of plots competing for the reader's moral attention. There is the poverty-stricken curate accused of theft; his daughter's love for the Archdeacon's son; the continued saga of John Eames's courtship of Lily Dale; and the problems of the artist Conway Dalrymple, making his way among the parvenus in London. These constitute the moral centres which compete for the reader's sympathy and judgement. The fundamental design is made by parallel and antithesis of character as well as by the similarity and contrast of the human situation. And it is essential for the reader to grasp these relations in order to follow Trollope's narrative in its fullest moral sense.

The Last Chronicle of Barset is a study of the possibilities for moral heroism in a world of fluctuating ideals and as such it is the exception to Trollope's consistent refusal, on the grounds of realism, to admit heroes into his fiction.[5] He feared the spread of bureaucracy and the commercial ethic and felt that the modern world, with its restrictive codes, its shifting ethical standards and corrupting pursuit of money had shrunk spiritually and offered little scope for acts of individual heroism.[6] However, Trollope still had faith in the sustaining and civilizing power of traditional cultural values fostered by the Church, by the rural community and by a strong literary heritage. He felt also that heroes were more than ever needed; not in the Carlylean mould, nor the Biedermeier heroes of cheap Victorian fiction, but as individuals who possessed the rare and peculiar kind of moral heroism which such traditional values help to shape. This is the unifying theme which informs Trollope's sophisticated narrative design. The form of *The Last Chronicle of Barset* is, I think, both more complex and more precisely articulated than Trollope has been given credit for and it is also the product of a more profoundly moral intelligence than Trollope has usually been allowed.

The major unifying characters of *The Last Chronicle of Barset*, Mr Crawley and John Eames, consistently advance its central moral concern as each in his way attempts to be a modern hero. The complete social and personal contrast between the ascetic country curate and the complacent young London civil servant, who never meet in the novel, draws attention to their parallel stories. At the conclusion Trollope makes it clear that it was not his intention to write 'an epic about clergymen'. Had this been his aim, he would have taken 'St Paul for [his] model' (II, 452). But in Mr Crawley's despairing battles with poverty, the law and the Church this is exactly the pattern of heroic martyrdom that he proposes to himself. It is part of his belief and part of his nature. His reading of the Greek drama and his identification with the great deliverer 'Eyeless in Gaza, at the mill with slaves' (II, 232) give him the inspiration he needs to prosecute a satisfying victory over the timid Bishop and his termagant wife. The battle for his pulpit makes the curate something of a hero in Barsetshire, but what spoils his claim to epic heroism is the rooted egoism that makes the image of a martyr attractive to him.[7] While Mr Crawley is making a stand against the foundering ideals of the Church, Eames's more limited idealism is expressed in his romantic constancy to Lily Dale, which bestows on him the conscious role of a 'hero of romance' (II, 322). This is given spurious substance in London by the myths, current at the Income-tax Board where he works, that have grown out of his thrashing of his rival Crosbie, so that 'Mr. John Eames had about him much of the heroic' (I, 147). In Barsetshire Mr Crawley is a poor and faintly silly figure, humbling his finely-honed intellect in the service of the Hoggle End labourers, while Eames, floating emotionally between the values of London and those of Barsetshire, accommodates himself uneasily to the insistently commercial ethos of the metropolis.

There is a pointed difference between the great epic heroes from whom Mr Crawley derives his strength and the potential heroes of *The Last Chronicle of Barset*. Since Victorian social life no longer offers the opportunity for heroism on a meaningful scale Trollope shows how, instead of the hero mirroring and amplifying the aspirations of his society, in contemporary life the potential hero has to battle against its collective will. The presence in this novel of idealistic rebels in conflict with major Victorian institutions and codes makes a large moral generalization. The political nature of ecclesiastical life is ironically exposed by the integrity of the curate's revolt. Belief in the sanctity of the priesthood dictates his cumulative battles and as sides are taken the schism in the diocese widens. This forms part of a larger pattern in the novel, for while the Church in Barsetshire is ruled by a weak, hen-pecked bishop, the Income-tax Board in London is run by the arrogant bully Sir Raffle Buffle. John Eames, his private secretary, resents his sycophantic position. He cannot be bothered to preserve the insidious illusion of industry that Buffle's ego demands. The superbly farcical scene in which Eames counterbluffs his superior in order to gain leave of absence to aid Mr Crawley makes a fine parallel with the curate's climactic interview at the palace, where Mr Crawley's equally shrewd political instinct quickly discerns and challenges the real source of diocesan power.

Rebellion is one of the counterpointed themes which bind the story. The major ironic effect of these scenes is that the true rebel in each case is the figurehead of the institution being threatened. Buffle's blatant abuse of power is an open secret in the Civil Service, which nevertheless allows him to retain his position, while the 'inhibition' that Mrs Proudie makes her husband send Mr Crawley is strictly illegal. As everyone in the diocese knows, the subversive force in Barsetshire is not the rebellious curate, but the Bishop's wife. There is a similarity of situation, but there is a difference of moral emphasis. Eames attacks the bureaucratic heavy-weight of the Civil Service from the strength conferred by his financial independence, while the curate has to construct his rebellion from political weakness and poverty; but Mr Crawley's revolt is in truth sincerely con-servative, while Eames's insouciant rebellion differs only in degree from his superior's self-regarding pride. Egoism is the root of moral failure in The Last Chronicle of Barset. This is illumined by the cluster of minor figures. Neither Mr Crawley's quest for sympathy among the labourers at Hoggle End nor Eames's soliciting of support from his wealthy patroness is in keeping with the demands of heroic dignity. What is more, the curate's relinquishing of his pulpit is the deliberate choice of an unnecessary martyrdom. Pride makes Mr Crawley's best actions perverse and this is something of which he is partly aware. Ironi-cally, Eames also succumbs to his own kind of myth-making, falling into the clutches of an aggressive London girl and almost wilfully losing Lily Dale, who has come to love him as a man, if not as a god. The parallel though separate and discrete development of their stories makes a dominant structural irony, which serves the function of moral emphasis as the wheel of fortune turns for both men, as in a morality play. At the conclusion of the novel the romantic hero, rejected for the last time by Lily Dale after his 'epic' pursuit of the Dean, is left weeping over a rail in a deserted street. For Mr Crawley, however, life reveals a different solution. His battles arise partly from thwarted ambition, so his elevation from the stylized posture of a radical defender of the poor to the status of a vicar is appropriate and embarrassingly human.

This is only one of a number of interlocking relations which advance the novel's central concern against a complex, densely realized social background. Like Eames, Major Grantly fails to achieve heroic stature in spite of all his moral striving. Trapped between the claims of rank and romantic heroism, he gives in to social pressure; not to the disguised materialism of his father the Archdeacon, nor even to the approbation of his class, but to the more subtle power of the novel's women. They view Lily Dale's refusal of John Eames and the Archdeacon's battle with his son as a threat to the romantic feminine love code, which in turn masks a hard-headed devotion to marriage. Just as Eames allows the women to plead his cause with Lily, so too Major Grantly is persuaded by the collective feminine will of Barsetshire society. His equivocation is resolved by a conversation with the austere but warm-hearted schoolmistress Miss Prettyman, and by a parallel encounter in Silverbridge High Street with the subversive millionairess Mrs Thorne, whose contempt for timid conformity to social rules, brusque dismissal of the affair of the 'trumpery cheque' and frank delight in romantic sacrifice, bring the staid Major to the point of reluctant decision.

One function of the interwoven plots is to create a pattern of moral correspondence in the reader's mind through juxtaposition. The meeting of Eames and Grantly on the railway train down to Guestwick, as each journeys to propose to his respective young lady, effects a natural transition from London to Barsetshire. But more importantly, it is also the meeting of different lives. Trollope's plots are really different versions of the same human predicament and here they meet, as they are designed to do. The deft juxtaposition of the points of view of the two men in the railway carriage, each pretending to read but pondering instead the difficult endeavour ahead, probes their claims to romantic heroism. Trollope's tone and the reading direction in the chapter title, 'A Hero at Home', alert the reader to the fact that Eames is a little too self-conscious and rather weary of his fruitless role. Trollope's ironic deflation also extends to the Major who, unlike Eames, anticipates an easy victory, but is conscious at the same time of his sacrifice and is not relishing the 'task' before him. While Eames's journey is the result of his friend Dalrymple's taunting, Major Grantly's trip is prompted by the social skill of the Barsetshire ladies. Moreover, just as Eames's lapses from constancy follow the examples of London life, so the Major's devotion at Allington is inspired, not by his easy victory but by Grace Crawley's selfless refusal of him. As Trollope comments sardonically, 'Half at least of the noble deeds done in this world are due to emulation, rather than to the native nobility of the actors' (I, 314). The moral distinction between the two men comes out in their contrasted capacity to learn. Grantly accepts the reprimand to his narrow egoism, but Eames fails to understand that he simply lacks the kind of heroic qualities that Lily Dale demands and he remains trapped by his illusions. What the weight of the novel's social panorama obscures it is the function of such a deft juxtaposition of plots to reveal.

For much of the novel the lives of these two men, which crisscross and run parallel before diverging, chart similar successes and failures; but the spirited girls whom they pursue both achieve a quiet moral victory. Grace Crawley and Lily Dale have contrasted origins and destinies, but they share an acuteness of moral sensibility which makes marriage problematical for them. And it prompts them to seek perversely heroic solutions to their dilemmas. Grace's sheltered life at the Hogglestock parsonage sharpens her suffering under the stigma of theft which her father has incurred. Nevertheless when Major Grantly finally proposes, she rejects the social approbation that such a marriage would confer on her disgraced family, feeling that her motives must be clearly above suspicion. For Lily Dale, who is older, the moral issue is more complex. In the past is her heartless jilting by Adolphus Crosbie; in the present is the choice between a tempting but dangerous marriage with him, or the social acclaim of a joyless match with John Eames. Her struggle to escape the illusions of her past is morally fine, but its conclusion is deliberately ambivalent.[8] Away from the security of her mother's house at Allington, Lily Dale is less pert, less wise too. The atmosphere of the metropolis, with its suggestion of new standards and wider possibilities, is morally unsettling. It makes correct decisions difficult. The London scenes are therefore all scenes of crisis for Lily Dale just as those in Barsetshire are for Grace Crawley. London is the place of her disenchantment as her encounters with Crosbie at the picture-gallery and in the park force her to accept how shabby her 'Pall Mall hero' really is. She cannot accept either man as hero or husband. In reaching this decision her adolescent egoism is gradually transmuted into the sustaining pride of self-denial and self-conquest. There is, Trollope suggests, something heroic in her final endorsement of the letters 'O.M.' in her book, but there is also something perverse and human.

The continuing story of John Eames and Lily Dale bulks large in *The Last Chronicle of Barset* because part of its function is to link the contrasted worlds of Barsetshire and London. In Barsetshire the illusory claims of epic and romantic heroism are soon discredited. They cannot flourish in a healthy moral climate. But in London people inhabit a world of fantasy. Here the unknown artist Conway Dalrymple, who deifies on canvas the leaders of the commercial world, becomes a celebrity overnight. The hero of the 'city' and the 'artist hero' are both the focus of society's escapist and perverted quest for romantic ideals. Here in the metropolis a further minor parallel is made between Dalrymple and John Eames. Eames's languid self-approval incurs heavy authorial irony as he is introduced as 'our hero' whose heroism lies merely in the fact that he moves among 'very respectable people' (I, 243). Dalrymple and Eames both employ their heroic roles to make a misplaced assault on the inner sanctum of this society; but through inexperience the young innocents are ensnared by its destructively neurotic women. Dalrymple quickly tires of the shallow, theatrical Mrs Dobbs Broughton while Eames, initially the more critical of the Broughton set, is completely beguiled by the wily, sophisticated Madalina Demolines.

The first fourteen chapters of *The Last Chronicle of Barset* read as if it were a novel with a central figure, concerned solely with Mr Crawley and the moral dilemma created by his supposed theft of Lord Lufton's cheque. By Chapter XIV rumour has spread and Barsetshire is alive with clerical scandal. Then the story moves rather abruptly from the curate to John Eames and the narrative never returns to Mr Crawley with quite the same concentration. His private agony takes its place in the rotating pattern of the other plots. The reader who desires tragedy may be disappointed by this movement, but it is strictly functional and its aim is the achievement of a realistic treatment of human issues. The obscure country curate cannot become a tragic St Paul figure in the modern world. His life has to be placed in perspective by the wider milieux of London so that it is swallowed up and forgotten in the bustle of the larger commercial and social world.

Trollope employs the techniques associated with multiple plotting to create structural effects that bind the story while permitting it to expand. This involves him in problems of transition, which are overcome by cross-cutting from one world to another. This makes for formal emphasis while stressing human variety. The first major transition from Barsetshire to the metropolis, the cross-cutting from the private scene at Allington between Lily Dale and her mother, with its fullness of human sympathy, to the public vulgarity of the Broughtons' dinner-party in Chapter XXIV is deliberately abrupt, morally complete and achieved with just the right modulation of narrative tone. Trollope's sympathy for Lily Dale's brave confrontation of her fear of moral cowardice contrasts with his sharp condemnation of Eames's smug acceptance of shoddy London ways. The transition, which is carefully related to plot and character, is made through the silent presence in the scene of Lily's agony of the two rivals, the would-be hero of romance, John Eames, and her former 'Apollo', Adolphus Crosbie. This relation is neatly reversed in the following scene at the Bayswater party where she makes a powerful impact on their hostile encounter, and both are ironically unaware of her decision to renounce them.

This patterning of interwoven plots and milieux produces a series of moving contrasts which gives *The Last Chronicle of Barset* its social richness and moral density. It also acts as a formal correlative for Trollope's apprehension of the shared surface of human life and creates an appropriate form for his investigation of a whole society. Since the hero is essentially an isolated figure, it is the crowdedness of the social world which often conceals from him the ironic correspondence of his predicament with those of other people. Mr Crawley, for instance, knows nothing of the poverty of Mr Quiverful. Moreover, the proximity of parallel lives can offer alternative examples to follow or reject. For Grace Crawley, the Miss Prettymans' lives as schoolmistresses, lonely and tainted with sexual and social failure, present the alternative to marriage. This is why they press her courtship with such vigour and agonize over her selfless refusal of Major Grantly. While for Lily Dale there is constantly before her the pre-nuptial joy of Emily Dunstable, which tempts her to salvage some happiness for herself in a marriage with John Eames. And what enhances the integrity of the moral choices of Grace and Lily is their quiet but stubborn refusal of easy alternatives.

Trollope also insists that heroic action must be viewed realistically in the context of life's limiting conditions of time and chance. Life offers various options which become irrevocable as past choices alter the present and also serve to make present comparisons. While, for Eames, Crosbie's presence in London gives continued support to his feeling of heroic dominance over the man he once thrashed, it is also a nagging reminder of his failure to achieve heroic stature in Lily Dale's terms. And in the same way, Dean Arabin forms part of the conscious burden of worldly failure that Mr Crawley has to bear. The reversal that has taken place in the lives of the Dean and the curate is, of course, one aspect of Trollope's criticism of the Church. While both were fine scholars at the university, in the political world of the Church one rose and the other fell. But this is also partly why one is a potential hero and the other is not. The intervening years of disappointment and frustration have nurtured Mr Crawley's revolutionary zeal, while the Dean has slipped into well-bred sloth. Indeed, Dean Arabin's success represents only one of a series of paths that were open to Mr Crawley, as his triumphant interview with the Bishop and his temperamental similarity to the Rural Dean Dr Tempest suggest. The curate is himself aware of this and it provides more fuel for his rebellion, for the kinds of lives which he covets and which might have been his, are precisely those lives that he feels morally compelled to shun. Not all Trollope's connections are as emphatic as this or we would lose the sense of naturalness which *The Last Chronicle of Barset* so richly provides, but they are strong enough to give a sense of unity in diversity, which is one of its dominant moral effects. The presentation of similar lives with different endings is a fundamental aspect of Trollope's realistic and moral sense. It places moral heroism firmly in the context of the variability of human growth and the continual narrowing of present choices.

Several critics dislike the shift in focus away from the story of Mr Crawley, the disreputable nature of the new characters who are introduced and the change in tone from the tragic to the satirical. However, this movement is thematically important. Barsetshire and London are clearly segregated areas of moral experience. The supposed theft of the cheque is a big scandal in Barsetshire, while in London thieving clergymen are almost commonplace. And similarly, Barsetshire's definitions of heroism and those of London are very different and must be allowed to comment on each other, especially since, as Trollope observes, metropolitan life is beginning to alter the country ways. He therefore insinuates into the narrative, quietly and without strain, many connections between Barsetshire and London. And in the modern world the strongest link is financial. Archdeacon Grantly draws a substantial income from London property; his son Charles preaches at a famous London church; Mrs Thorne's ointment millions allow her to keep an ostentatious house there and Eames's legacy assists him to prosper in London in the Civil Service. In Barchester the palace is invaded by evangelical Londoners and the ancient cathedral close is threatened by the desecrating hands of the Ecclesiastical Commission. The influence of metropolitan values is extended as London increasingly becomes the source of Barsetshire wealth and power and as it meddles more and more in provincial affairs.

Part of the contrast between the two worlds is made in scenes which overlap in time, thus drawing them to the surface of the reader's moral attention. As Eames's trip to Barsetshire coincides with Mr Crawley's visit to London, the potential hero of Barsetshire is being tried by the hard-headed reality of the city, while the romantic hero of the metropolis is being tested by the moral context of the country. The bewildered Mr Crawley is engaged on a painful quest for the truth of his moral condition and in baring his heart to the vulgar, shrewd, but generous lawyer, Mr Toogood, the shy and fastidious curate undergoes a penitential exercise in humility. The setting of Eames's crisis at Allington is more quietly emblematic. The frosted garden of the Small House makes an image of the dead relation with Lily Dale which he refuses to recognize. The strength and tact with which Lily rejects her opportunity to avoid the blight of spinsterhood means that Allington comes to stand in the novel as the emblem of the country's power of almost too self-conscious moral scrutiny. Eames returns to London with the knowledge that he is 'vain, and foolish, and unsteady' (I, 372), but its unreal atmosphere quickly absorbs him once again and he manages to turn failure into romantic martyrdom on an 'heroic' scale.

In the pattern of interwoven plots an important effect, as one plot is replaced with another, is structural irony. This is especially powerful in the cross-cutting between Chapters XL and XLI, from Mr Toogood's aggressively homely hospitality in London to Mr Crawley's ill health at Hogglestock. Here Trollope relies on the power of gossip and rumour, the connecting and relating agents *in The Last Chronicle of Barset*, to assist the transition. Mr Toogood defends Mr Crawley before the urbane Silverbridge attorney Mr Walker, but he is forced to admit the justice of the popular opinion that the curate is a 'queer fish' (I. 414). The subsequent shift in scene to the curate's house is a movement from the city to the country, from city affluence to an interior marked by poverty and from the measured tone of professional debate to the human agony. Neither man has seen him like this. Prostrated by the journey to London and by overwork, his delirious revelation of the truth about the missing cheque spills out unremarked. This demonstrates how Mr Crawley's queerness, his inability to recall money given in charity, is part of his heroic strength as well as one aspect of his human failure. Because the crowd scene is segregated from that in which the curate is presented in isolation the reader turns with greater sympathy from the misunderstanding group to the scarcely-known man. Since, as the novel demonstrates, heroes nowadays are 'queer', public discussion obscures their private suffering, just as rumour makes what is private public and unbearable.

The most important effect of the pattern of rotating plots in *The Last Chronicle of Barset* is the deliberate ironic undercutting of one story by the next. Eames's shallow heroics are set beside the greater generosity of Major Grantly and their limited rebellions are in turn undercut by the tenacity of Mr Crawley's courageous revolt against the Bishop. It is a complex moral design which reveals only finally their complete moral stature. We discover with a shock that Mr Crawley's revolutionary fervour and intellectual arrogance overlie an innate conservatism and humility of almost heroic magnitude. When Mr Toogood and Major Grantly bring news that he will not now have to stand trial, the curate astounds them by remarking that in his clearer moments he had known all along where the cheque came from. What his pride and jealousy have concealed is that he really does believe in the superiority of Dean Arabin and was too humble to contradict his friend for a second time. When Major Grantly exclaims 'I call that man a hero' (II, 354) it is difficult not to agree. Even worldly Mr Toogood does. But it is a heroism qualified by the development of the novel as a whole and by Mr Crawley's assimilation at its conclusion into the easier conventions of polite ecclesiastical society as he is transformed into an establishment figure.

This process of deferred judgement is partly due to the progress and treatment of character. Our interest in Mr Crawley involves a changed response to him as he alters under the impact of political strife from a self-pitying, maudlin figure to a formidable rebel. However, all the claimants to a degree of moral heroism present different versions of failure when they are set beside the gracious humility of old Mr Harding, who emerges as the novel's most consistent rebel and its only true moral hero. This dominant irony, which Trollope allows to surface late in the novel, is deliberately concealed by the bustle of the various stories competing for our attention, all of which are finally set beside that of Mr Harding to be judged. Trollope's hero is an odd, saintly old man, simple, selfless and apparently ignored in all diocesan affairs. But he possesses to a profound degree the quality of sympathy which is such a healing force in Trollope's divided world. Just as in *The Warden*, when he battled successfully with his powerful, bullying son-in-law the Archdeacon over relinquishing Hiram's Hospital, and in *Barchester Towers*, when with rare political shrewdness and love for the Church he renounced the deanery in favour of Arabin, he is still a tenacious though sweet-tempered rebel. In *The Last Chronicle of Barset* he triumphs not only over his worldly daughter, for he thinks highly of Grace Crawley, but over the whole diocese because he is almost alone in refusing to believe that a Barsetshire clergyman could be a thief. And he strenuously asserts Mr Crawley's innocence in the teeth of all the evidence, risking ridicule as a senile and foolish old man.

Mr Harding represents Trollope's ideal of heroic goodness. He has unlimited faith in the Church and in humanity. It is his sympathy for Mr Crawley which prompts the letter to his daughter Eleanor, the Dean's wife, that finally discloses the origin of the cheque. It is Mr Harding's profound sympathy and clarity of moral vision that allows him to discern and remedy the cause of Mr Crawley's martyrdom and he is the source of the profound reversal of fortune in Mr Crawley's life. His last and most selfless act is that of ensuring that his own living, St Ewold's Parsonage, will go after his death to the curate whom he has scarcely known, but in whom he has recognized those marks of spiritual distinction needed in the higher service of the Church. In the scene at Mr Harding's death-bed, with its marvellously controlled pathos, his moral influence over the bluff Archdeacon is so strong that St Ewold's is promised for Mr Crawley with a squeeze of the hand. The origin of the old man's moral power lies in his complete unworldliness and in the unfeigned love that people bear him. With a few quiet words he contrives to close the breach between Henry Grantly and his father. And even after his death he is still a pervasive presence whose healing power is at work in human lives. The Bishop remembers him as the only person in the diocese who genuinely mourned the death of Mrs Proudie and his presence at Mr Harding's funeral prompts the Archdeacon's surprising inward pledge of future peace in the diocese. This healing web of profoundly emotional responses to the moral presence of the old man repairs the fabric of human life in Barchester. In a strange way Mr Harding's moral heroism also invariably produces the shrewdest and healthiest political solutions. Grantly is profoundly moved by the death of his old friend. Pacing before the deanery fire, in a rare moment of moral insight there bursts from him the alien judgement that the odd old man he had often scorned had 'all the spirit of a hero' (II, 421). This revelation has all the weight of the novel's structure behind it; for Trollope places it at the centre of a number of interlocking stories and allows it to emerge late in the narrative with the maximum of ironic effect. He is concerned to show that in an increasingly materialistic, political and self-absorbed society the truly effective revolutionary is a conservative and a man with no pride. The moral hero of *The Last Chronicle of Barset* is the 'unheroic' hero.

The movement away to London a third of the way through the novel means that such heroism is placed in a much wider social context. Trollope wishes to demonstrate how the decline of moral heroism is connected with the spread of materialism and the corresponding loss of human scale in modern life. For much of the novel's length the technique of balance and counter-point is employed to advance this vision. The shifts from the country to London and back are made in terms of the moral atmosphere of places like the open fields of Allington which is the setting of Lily Dale's self-sacrifice and an emblem of the country's power of moral discrimination; or the secretiveness of dingy Hook Court, the origin of Dobbs Broughton's tinsel splendour and the scene of his suicide. These places can bear the weight of emblematic significance for the lives of the people who live there because they are first realized on a physical and human level. One powerful effect of the contrapuntal structure of the London and Barsetshire plots lies in Trollope's emblematic use of scenes which take their place in the balancing masses of the novel. In particular he employs two such scenes to show how the focus of idealizing tendencies in modern times has changed; it is no longer the local parson as it was in the days of Jane Austen, but the city financier. The occasion of the drinking of the last of the 1820 port at Plumstead is, for old Mr Harding, an occasion for quiet nostalgia for the days when clergymen were gentlemen; when they danced and played cards. But when the Archdeacon makes this a source of bitter contrast with the present, Mr Harding's scrupulous conscience forces him to take a radical stance and denounce the idleness of former days. Nevertheless, the drinking of the wine confers an almost sacra-mental quality upon the past, which is intensified by their acute sense of mutability. The corresponding scene at the Broughtons' dinner-party is in striking contrast as we move from the clergy-men's quiet conversation to the forced gaiety and concealed tensions of the secular world of Bayswater. There is a complete change of tone as Broughton vulgarly boasts of the price of his '42 Bordeaux. For him it merely represents success, and is part of his posture as a hero of materialism. Here in the contrast between Barsetshire and London the emblematic patterning of the ecclesiastical and the secular, the past and the present, is full and complete.

These emblems are local and temporary, but there are two emblems which Trollope employs recurrently: the painting of Jael and Sisera on which the artist Dalrymple is engaged, and

Mr Crawley's books. The painting functions as a metaphor for the London scenes as the books do for those in Barsetshire. They indicate how the achievement of some kind of moral heroism depends on people retaining links with a strong cultural tradition. The painting represents the perversion of art and history, for Dalrymple is simply pandering to the commercial man's desire to attain a kind of heroic immortality. More significantly, like Sisera the London men are betrayed into the treacherous hands of rapacious women and the dominance of the female will marks this society as neurotic and nihilistic. The grotesque scenes at the Broughtons' house serve cumulatively to extend the meaning of the picture, which becomes suddenly explicit when Dalrymple rips it apart in the presence of Mrs Van Siever. He does so because he recognizes that its absurd illusion gets in the way of human reality and by this action he asserts his preference for the sober honesty of Clara Van Siever, even with her poverty, to the sham heroism conferred on him by art and wealth. It is a small heroic gesture, but one which Trollope shows is increasingly difficult to make in the modern world.

As I have already suggested here, Trollope retained a strongly held faith in the sustaining moral force of a cultural heritage. And while culture is prostituted in London, what fortifies Mr Crawley, by contrast, in his battles against an oppressive world are his tattered books of heroic mythology. After the challenging visit of Mr Thumble with the Bishop's 'inhibition' the curate returns to a zestful examination of *The Seven Against Thebes*. Mr Crawley conceives of his martyrdom in heroic as well as in Christian terms and he identifies strongly with heroic figures. Yet he talks disparagingly of *Samson Agonistes* – 'Agonistes indeed!' (II, 232). Even with the support of an intellectual tradition, in Trollope's balanced and realistic view moral heroism is still a human and fallible affair.

The novel's emblematic pattern also extends to the sphere of money. Trollope's potential heroes all strive to combat the crushing pressures of bureaucracy and rigid social attitudes, but they struggle hardest against the corrupting power of cash. Again there is no hiatus between the realistic surface of the novel and its metaphorical significance. In Barsetshire Lord

Lufton's missing cheque gives an initial impetus to the story, but thereafter its main function is emblematic. It stands for the worldliness of Barsetshire and its poorest curate's ignorance of financial affairs, but it also charts the moral movement in the country, which is to care less about the cheque and more about the welfare of Mr Crawley and his family. The worldliness of London, in Trollope's view, has reached irredeemable proportions. Here people are linked only by commercial bills. Emblems of trust in the business world, ironically they become the focus of intrigue and revenge. The origin of Broughton's wealth, they pay for his wife's romantic fantasies; they are the cause of his suicide and they finally ruin Crosbie and Musselboro. These elusive commercial bills, with their power to blight and destroy, form the shifting base of a rootless society. And in *The Last Chronicle of Barset* Trollope uses them to mark the end of the intimate, morally vital world of *The Warden* and to foreshadow his horrifying vision of the nihilistic world of *The Way We Live Now*.

The Last Chronicle of Barset possesses a remarkable depth of temporal and moral perspective, and this is bestowed on it by Trollope's unique use of time. His introduction of all the major figures of the Barsetshire novels is not simply his means of taking an elaborate farewell of them, as some critics have suggested. Rather, he examines their moral development in order to see whether his generalizations about humanity hold true. And he makes this daring perspective entirely relevant to his central moral concern, as life offers them a second chance to affirm or deny their moral directions. For instance, Lady Lufton's fear of her son's entanglement with the socially insignificant Lucy Robarts in *Framley Parsonage* is repeated in the lives of Archdeacon Grantly and Grace Crawley, a situation on which Lady Lufton's advice is sought. She has plainly learned from her earlier experience and the Archdeacon and Grace profit from her generous and rebellious modernity. Similarly, John Eames's heroism in *The Small House at Allington* where he thrashed Crosbie and saved Earl De Guest from a bull, is fully tried in *The Last Chronicle of Barset* and is found to be badly flawed by egoism. Lily Dale on the other hand, learns from her juvenile infatuation and in this novel achieves a perversely heroic triumph, but it is a triumph heavily qualified by Trollope's measured irony: 'My old friend John was certainly no hero, – was very unheroic in many phases of his life; but then, if all the girls are to wait for heroes, I fear that the difficulties in the way of matrimonial arrangements, great as they are at present, will be very seriously enhanced' (II, 371). The most obvious instance of this kind of repeated situation is the testing of Mrs Proudie's egoism, since her encounters with Mr Crawley and Dr Tempest exceed her comic interference in *Barchester Towers*. She possesses Mr Crawley's heroic power of will, but in her it has become a purely destructive force and she has to die. But most important is the manner in which, for old Mr Harding, his past is repeated in the Bishop's hounding of Mr Crawley, which recalls his own past moral battles over Hiram's Hospital. Like Mr Crawley, Mr Harding in *The Warden* also made a painful journey to London to consult a disinterested lawyer about a delicate moral dilemma and he likewise decided, after examining his conscience, on a course of humble submission. Mr Crawley is exhorted by Dr Tempest not to relinquish his living for the sake of a mere ideal, just as Mr Harding was harangued by the Archdeacon for his absurd scrupulosity. And Mr Harding's determined and generous response to Mr Crawley's predicament in this novel affirms the moral parallel.

In his portrayal of Mr Crawley and Mr Harding in *The Last Chronicle of Barset*, Trollope reveals simultaneously his admiration for the revolutionary heroic ideal and his awareness of the need for a conservative, sustaining cultural context. Carlyle's response to the new, unheroic, materialistic age, was to turn in *Past and Present* to the social values of the Middle Ages. But Trollope's past extends only as far as the world of Jane Austen and the youth of Mr Harding, which is evoked in the drinking of the port. The end of the era of *The Warden* is realized emblematically in Mr Harding's violoncello. Like Mr Crawley's books, it is an appropriate emblem for a supporting culture, but its function is also quieter and more personal and denotes, for Trollope, the quintessentially heroic. What it comes to signify is given in the scene in which his tiny granddaughter

Posy succeeds in getting weird melodies from its ancient strings, while Mr Harding recalls the earlier days when he played to the fractious bedesmen in the idyllic garden of Hiram's Hospital. Mr Harding has been a creative moral force in people's lives, a healing, unifying power in society, and the emblem of the child playing on his violoncello represents Trollope's hope for the continued functioning of innocence and harmony in human relations. For Trollope this is the task of the moral hero and in *The Last Chronicle of Barset* he employs the story in one of its most complex forms to examine the paradox that in the modern world, true revolutionary moral heroism is rooted in a Christian spirit of humility and self-sacrifice.

The Closed Form: Trollope's Experimental Novels

Trollope's short novels, as Ruth apRoberts has pointed out, are important to the critic interested in the form of his fiction.[9] However, those novels which he wrote anonymously at the peak of his fame in the 1860s have been virtually ignored.[10] But they are of particular interest because, standing cheek by jowl in the long list of Trollope's fiction with broad studies of the Victorian social milieu like *The Last Chronicle of Barset* and wide-ranging socio-political novels like *Phineas Finn*, which are in general balanced, relatively sanguine books, these short, intense, bleakly deterministic novels represent, in my view, Trollope's endeavour to significantly modify the mode of realism that he had established by the early 1860s and to articulate once more the tragic philosophy of life which dominates his earliest novel, *The Macdermots of Ballycloran*. These novels thus express the darker side of Trollope's mind, which for the most part he had hitherto kept strictly under control.

As his deliberate decision to bring the Barsetshire series to a close indicates, Trollope felt that he had reached a watershed in his fiction. He realized increasingly, as he makes clear in his *Autobiography*, that his growing interest in the psychology of character rather than in social commentary demanded a different form. In the novels of the 1860s we find, for instance, several potentially tragic figures like Lady Mason, Hugh Clavering, Mr Crawley or Mr Kennedy, whose inner lives often occupy an important place in the novels, but whose individual tragedies are engulfed by Trollope's overwhelming social preoccupations. By contrast, in his experimental novels as I have called them, *Nina Balatka, Linda Tressel, The Golden Lion of Granpère* and *An Eye for An Eye*, Trollope wanted to penetrate beneath the façade of social manners, the nexus of roles, rules, laws and attitudes which govern our social responses, in order to explore their complex psychological causes and frequently tragic effects. And he also introduces something which had virtually disappeared from his fiction since *The Macdermots of Ballycloran*, the vision of human lives as being subject to fate. This is clear if we compare his treatment of Mr Crawley with that of Nina Balatka, Linda Tressel or Fred Neville. In a fundamental sense Mr Crawley's character can be regarded as his destiny: the proud curate's fate is to a great extent in his own hands and we watch him choosing freely both his initial rebellion and his later submission to authority. The world of *Nina Balatka* is ruled by the dead weight of history, which is only narrowly thwarted by unpredictable impulses of human generosity; while in *An Eye for An Eye* blind fate governs the lives of all the characters and finally overwhelms the novel's central figure, Fred Neville.

In particular, *Linda Tressel*, Trollope's second anonymous novel and a powerful and gloomy book, reveals his interest in abnormal psychology and his new fatalism. Linda's destiny is shaped both by her character and by social circumstance. Her crime is that she falls in love with a young revolutionary Ludovic Valcarm, and she is therefore relentlessly persecuted by her Calvinist aunt, in whom Trollope explores the corrosive effects of religious fanaticism: 'To Madame Staubach's mind a broken heart and a contrite spirit were pretty much the same thing. It was good that hearts should be broken, that all the inner humanities of the living being should be, as it were, crushed on a wheel and ground into fragments, so that nothing should be left capable of receiving pleasure from the delights of the world' (p. 294). As her instrument of oppression Madame Staubach chooses her dull, middle-aged lodger Peter Steinmarc, but when Linda runs away from him, horrified at the prospect of such a marriage, he too reveals a strong sadistic streak: 'He wanted to be her master, to get the better of her, to punish her for her disdain of him, and to bring her to his feet' (p. 350). Indeed, Linda's whole society becomes her adversary; for even when she flees to her dead father's old friend Herr Molk, as soon as he learns the identity of her anarchic lover, he too joins in the condemnation. However, Linda cannot escape with Valcarm because she is torn between her profound need for love and sympathy and her conviction of guilt, the result of the prolonged religious indoctrination which has rendered her weak and submissive. This deep psychological torment emerges symbolically in her dreams about Valcarm, who would come to her 'beautifully, like an angel, and, running to her in her difficulties, dispersed all her troubles by the beauty of his presence. But then the scene would change, and he would become a fiend instead of a god, or a fallen angel; and at those moments it would become her fate to be carried off with him into uttermost darkness' (pp. 250–1). Linda cannot free herself from the tyranny of her aunt's peculiar religion: 'The doctrine had been taught her from her youth upwards, and she had not realized the fact that she possessed any power of rejecting it' (pp. 362–3). And once she accepts the degree to which her character and her life have been thus determined, the only logical resolution of her dilemma is death.

The corollary of Trollope's decision to dramatize more intensively the psychology of his characters and the operation of an unremitting fate was the necessity of experimenting with a different form. He had to make a break with the multi-plotted novel with its gallery of figures and several centres of interest and return to the 'closed' form of the single-plot novel, a form even more tightly and logically articulated than a carefully developed situation such as we find, for instance, in *The Warden*. And the taut structure of *Nina Balatka* and *Linda Tressel*, together with the lists of dramatis personae which Trollope, unusually, gives us at the beginning of these novels, suggests to me that he was conscious of their affinity with the drama.

The question that has teased Trollope readers for so long is why he should have chosen to publish these novels anonymously. Trollope's own explanation of such a daring venture at the height of his popularity and just two months after his attack on the pernicious practice of anonymity in the *Fortnightly Review* has never seemed to me to be very convincing. According to Trollope, writing in his *Autobiography*, by the mid-1860s he was a rich and successful novelist and wondered whether 'a name once earned carried with it too much favour'. He set out, therefore, to test the hypothesis that it was an author's name rather than the value of his work that attracted the reading public to a new novel and he decided 'to begin a course of novels anonymously'.[11] I think that there is some truth in R. C. Terry's view that this unusual experiment is yet another instance of Trollope's continual need to prove himself;[12] but the main reason, it seems to me, has to do with the nature of the novels, and Trollope himself, in his *Autobiography*, draws our attention to their unusual features: their foreign settings, local colouring, elements of romance and their pathos. He speaks of these as hallmarks of his new identity as a writer, but just as the roles of disinterested liberal and unintellectual storyteller are two of the many masks that Trollope employs in the *Autobiography* to shield himself from possible criticism, or even ridicule, so too, in my view, is the whole question of identity. On the practical level, he knew that his reputation rested on the splendid social comedy of the Barsetshire novels and naturally enough he was unwilling to risk alienating his faithful readers by making a sudden and dramatic change of style under his own name, although his identity was quickly discovered by Richard Holt Hutton who reviewed *Nina Balatka* in the *Spectator*. But the fundamental reason for his decision to publish anonymously lay, I believe, in his dissatisfaction with the mode and form of his realistic fiction in the 1860s, and the cloak of anonymity, which freed him both from critical hostility and from obligations to his regular readers, allowed him the scope to give full play to his tragic vision, to experiment with psychological realism and to develop a different form in which to articulate it.

Although *An Eye For An Eye* was finally published in 1879 with Trollope's name on the title page, like *The Golden Lion of Granpère*, I include it with *Nina Balatka* and *Linda Tressel* because in addition to being written roughly contemporaneously with them, it bears their unmistakable stamp. It explores intense social conflict rooted in religious divisions, incorporates a deterministic view of life and develops a single, tragic crisis which takes place in a foreign setting. Moreover, from a formal point of view it represents a development in Trollope's experiment with the 'closed' form of the novel. Bearing this in mind, its long-deferred publication, always something of a mystery to Trollope scholars, can be seen as probably due to the comparative failure of his earlier anonymous novels, for by the time he eventually decided to publish *An Eye for An Eye* the dramatic form of the novel had begun to find broader critical favour.

In my view then, taken together these novels represent a highly self-conscious attempt to transpose the form of the drama into fictional terms and as such they must be viewed in the context of Trollope's interest in contemporary critical theory. As Richard Stang has demonstrated, the mid-Victorian debate about dramatic construction and unity in the novel created a significant body of critical opinion in favour of more artistic rigour. Neo-classicists in particular, such as Trollope's friends G. H. Lewes and R. H. Hutton, preferred the 'closed' form of the intensively dramatic novel, although others such as Fitzjames Stephen and Charles Kingsley complained that theorists looked too much to the French well-made play for their model, rather than to the ampler form offered by Shakespeare.[13] In his experimental novels Trollope employed the criteria of economy, proportion, selection and unity advocated by Lewes and Hutton, but what is most striking about them is the way in which their single plots articulate so clearly both the nature of the dramatic conflict and the growth of its intense crisis. As on the stage, the conflict of opposed wills creates a correspondence of character and situation which is mirrored emblematically in the sharply contrapuntal arrangement of scene and setting, and the development of the crisis possesses a complementary temporal rhythm that gives to sequential interest a moral intensity. This places on Trollope the obligation to provide the kind of climactic scene which is rare in his novels, the function of which is to resolve the crisis and reveal its full significance and the justification for which lies in the concentration and economy demanded of the 'closed' form.

The change in Trollope's stance as a realist in *Nina Balatka* is due in no small measure to the influence of G. H. Lewes. The novel was written in 1865 immediately after Trollope's return from Prague, which Lewes had visited earlier and which inspired the central illustration in his well-known article on art as a means of discovering the Ideal in the Real:

We remember walking through the Jews' quarter in Prague, when it had for us only a squalid curiosity, until the sight of a cheap flower or two in the windows, and a dirty Jew fondling his baby, suddenly shed a beam as of sunlight over the squalor, and let us into the secret of the human life there. The artist who depicted only what we saw at first, would not have been so real as he who also depicted the flowers and affections; and not being so real, he would not have been so poetical.[14]

In *Nina Balatka* Trollope takes up Lewes's challenge to the realist to penetrate to the deeper relation between character and its social environment and he avoids novelistic cliché in his treatment of the Jews by evoking powerfully the deterministic ethos of the Prague ghetto but by revealing at the same time the deep-rooted humanity of its secret life, although in the end this works against his tragic vision.[15]

The novel's basic pattern derives from the stark nature of the tragic social schism in Prague between Jews and Christians. Whereas the Christians are marked by a crippling egoism fed by their traditional role as racial oppressors, the Jews, shackled by their ghetto spirit, are nevertheless torn between self-interest and social impulse. Trollope's general moral classification of character is evident in the broad contrast he makes between the kindly patriarch Stephen Trendellsohn and the gentile virago Madame Zamenoy; and between the Jews' treatment of the orphaned Ruth Jacobi, which stresses the communal caring engrained in Judaism, and the Christians' ostracism of their

relatives, old Balatka and his daughter, whom they have bank-
rupted. Trollope reveals a world of poisoned human relations,
and the racial conflict in the divided city shapes the novel's central moral concern: the intense struggle that takes place between
the contrary human impulses of fidelity and treachery, between
a tentative movement towards social integration and sheer brutal
nihilism. These forces are intensified in the lives of Anton, the
young Jewish visionary and his Christian fiancée Nina, whose
struggle to break out of the vicious circle of history and to
unite Prague by their marriage gives them important status at
the centre of the conflict.

Trollope's moral sense and his dramatic impulse reinforce
each other in a pattern of correspondence of character and
situation which reveals the ironic confusion of racial labels and
moral tags. Anton's mature, sacrificial love for Nina, which
threatens to alienate him from the other members of his race,
is opposed by the adolescent sexuality of his petulant Christian
rival, Ziska Zamenoy; while the Jewess Rebecca Loth's superbly
disinterested humanity contrasts with her rival Nina's more
limited and selfish love. However, Trollope's clear moral pattern
can shift. It does so, for instance, in the scene where Anton
stands looking up at the lamp in Nina's window while inside
she sits pondering the implications of her love for the Jew. As
in the theatre, it makes a split scene which provokes a spatial
reading and creates a collective image of inside and outside,
light and darkness, warmth and cold, that underlines Anton's
increasing isolation in the gloom of his engrained Jewish suspicion of the Christians. But Anton and Nina are only partly
representative of their respective factions. The moral contrast
between them – between his reluctant impulse towards
treachery and her tenacious affirmation of loyalty – is also a
fundamental aspect of their personal relation, and by thus revealing their full humanity Trollope emphasizes the deep irony
of their personal commitment. Trollope also seeks to overcome our conventional response to the moral conflict in another
way for, ironically, one of the most destructive elements at work
in the divided city is not stereotyped Jewish avarice, but the
bitterly competitive will of the Christians. The Zamenoys'

rampant materialism is reflected in their smart New Town suburban house, which is reached by straight, functional, ugly streets, while the Balatkas' home, hidden in a tangle of back-streets in the picturesque Kleinseite district, images the consequent imprisoning effect of their poverty.

Trollope's tragic sense of the clutch of history is also expressed in this novel by the unity of place which he achieves. Its characters are set in close proximity to one another in order to shape the action all the time, but in addition the social and geographical milieux of reactionary Prague create a significant counterpoint which defines emblematically and with great economy the broader context of racial strife. Just as the empty Hradschin Palace, peopled by Nina with happy lovers, rises in the moonlight out of Balatka's house, Nina's need of a sustaining illusion grows out of her social ostracism; but as a potent emblem of a repressive regime, the palace of the old kings of Bohemia places Nina's dreams of social integration in a deeply ironic perspective. And its parallel Jewish emblem, the ancient synagogue which similarly overshadows the Trendellsohns' house in the ghetto, and in the centre of which is 'a cage . . . within which five or six old Jews were placed, who seemed to wail louder than the others' (p. 84) focuses Trollope's view of Judaism as an inextricable tangle of religious faith and social history. The ghetto, like the Kleinseite, is a claustrophobic spiritual area and the synagogue with its cage, like the empty palace, functions as an emblem of the imprisoning forces of history from which Nina and Anton, on behalf of a whole generation, strive to free themselves.

Trollope's pessimistic view of the limited possibilities for meaningful social action is mirrored in the inevitability of the plot of *Nina Balatka*, each section of which is also a well-marked succession of crises, stimulating and satisfying an interest of their own while advancing the narrative. The first section defines the nature of the conflict in Prague and reveals how in the twelve short days following her engagement to Anton both factions spurn Nina; the second section, which covers the next twelve days in which they contrive to bring about her isolation and submission, culminates in Rebecca Loth's surprising visit to tempt Nina to take part with her in a joint sacrifice for Anton;[16] while the final section, spanning only four days, moves swiftly through Anton's treachery, old Balatka's death, Nina's complete social alienation, her attempted suicide and her rescue by the Jewess. But while time articulates the rhythm of the novel, it also bestows on it a measure of unity, emphasizing Trollope's profound sense of the tragic ironies possible in a world darkened by hatred. Nina's reflection at the beginning of the novel that her twenty-first birthday in a month's time will bring her freedom is balanced at its conclusion by her bitter reverie before her attempted suicide. The wedding day that she has been joyfully anticipating almost becomes the day of her death.

Time also repeats itself in a way that the reader recognizes, although the characters do not, as they are continually forced to re-emphasize their moral directions. As racial fears take on different guises Anton is tempted to forsake Nina, first by the Zamenoys' lies, then by Ziska Zamenoy's attempted bribery and finally by the misplaced zeal of Souchey, Nina's servant. Each time, in spite of himself, his suspicions harden and he moves further towards his act of betrayal. And similarly, Nina undergoes three separate periods of temptation to abandon her Jewish lover. There is Ziska Zamenoy's offer of marriage and social acceptance, her father's dire poverty and sickness and, finally, Rebecca Loth's subtly attractive temptation to make an idealistic gesture of renunciation of Anton as proof of her love for him. In the moral confusion that reigns in Prague, wrong courses can be pursued from the highest motives, but Nina recognizes Rebecca's proposal as fundamentally divisive and negative. However, in contrast to Anton's abject surrender to traditional racial fears, Nina's thrice-affirmed fidelity makes a striking parallel with the redemptive power of the Jewess's remarkable faithfulness in sending her forlorn Christian rival food and clothing and in appearing once more just in time to save her from suicide. In a similar way, the pattern made by Nina's three spiritual crises, which take place on the Moldau bridge that symbolically as well as physically links Jewish and Christian Prague, makes the larger generalization.

Her temptation to betray, as she believes, Christianity for Judaism, is defined in ironic terms for her by the statue of the Catholic saint, drowned for refusing to betray the secrets of a queen's confession. Each period of trial is resolved by Nina's clinging to her choice of a husband from among the Jews, but is also accompanied by the gradual unbalancing of her mind which leads with frightening logic to the inevitable final scene.

This scene, which is central to Trollope's careful exploration of Nina's tortured consciousness, reflects back on a whole series of events, for Nina's reverie on the bridge encapsulates the development of her obsession with suicide. As her progressive isolation from a caring world engenders unbearable feelings of spiritual alienation and guilt Lotta Luxa's malicious prediction that the Jew would jilt her, which is symptomatic of the mind-less hostility that infests Prague, becomes reinforced in Nina's mind as she reflects that Lotta's second prediction of suicide by drowning must also be fulfilled (p. 177). For Nina the river is no longer simply a divisive feature of the Prague landscape, but has become a personal, malignant force and an agent of the fate that Lotta Luxa has forseen. In her agony and confusion, suicide ap-pears to Nina at different moments to bestow personal, social and metaphysical significance on her wretched life. It is a re-venge on Anton, a perverted test of her capacity for fidelity, a spiritual quest, God's retribution and a personal atonement for the whole history of social evil in Prague. But her instinctive identification in her final moments of despair with St John of Nepomucene illumines both the fragility and the sanctity of simple human faith as the only worthwhile value in a torn world. However, it is not the saint's legendary power which saves Nina from becoming the tragic victim of historical forces, but the strenuous love of her Jewish rival, who ironically embodies the power and the function of the dead Christian saint, and whose final appearance as Nina's redeemer we have been led to antici-pate. By his pairing of these two women at the conclusion of the novel, Trollope stresses their totally sacrificial fidelity as repre-senting the only possible hope for social harmony. But Anton, corrupted by the ghetto mentality, recognizes this too late and, coming as it does after he has almost caused Nina's death, their reunion clearly provides an inadequate foundation upon which to build a new society.

The emphatic parallel which Trollope makes between the Jewess and the Christian, together with the hurried reconciliation between Anton and Nina and their exodus from Prague to seek a new life in a more tolerant society, are all huddled up in a brief epilogue, which produces a weakened and faulty ending to the novel. But this is not Trollope shirking tragedy, for the avoidance of a tragic conclusion has been foreshadowed. Rather, it proceeds from Trollope's artistic commitment to divided aims. He is attempting to reconcile Lewes's idealistic notion of the triumph of humane impulses over historical adversity, embodied particularly in Rebecca Loth, with his own deeply tragic instinct, expressed in his dramatization of the tortured psychology of Nina Balatka.[17] I believe it is of equal significance that it also stems in part from Trollope's acknowledgement of the law of dramatic economy, which as yet he had only imperfectly adapted to the novel.

However, in *An Eye for An Eye*, written in accordance with the strict neo-classical rules favoured by Hutton, who praised its simplicity and proportion,[18] Trollope allowed his gloomier vision full rein and produced a bleakly deterministic tragedy. From the beginning there is an almost Aeschylean sense of fate brooding over the protagonists as the absurd conflict between freedom and duty is developed by the rigidly schematic pattern of characters arranged in blindly hostile groups. The tragedy is dependent on the gulf that exists between England and Ireland, Protestants and Catholics, aristocrats and commoners, rich and poor. The Scroope family in Dorset and Mrs O'Hara and Father Marty in Ireland battle dourly for control of the will of Fred Neville, the novel's central character, in accordance with their differing notions of obligation, which the former see as his duty to an abstract, idealized conception of social rank, and the latter as his more particular human obligation to Kate O'Hara, who is expecting his child. The focus of the novel is the psychology of Neville, whose choice constitutes its crisis. And what gives him importance at the centre of its conflicting claims is his very ordinariness, for Trollope's tragic vision has none of the grandeur of heroic tragedy. He is introduced as a particular kind of chooser, who sees situations only in terms of black and white alternatives and who equivocates when events prove to be intractable. His romantic notions of freedom are shown to be pathetically inadequate in the context of the clashing fatal imperatives of the conflict, and he is murdered. Few plays, which by their nature aim at compression and concentration, attempt more than this and Trollope resolves his plot with dramatic lucidity and, I think, with genuine tragic power.

As in *Nina Balatka*, the reader's moral attention is economized by the selection of a few foreground characters. However, in *An Eye for An Eye* the conflict of wills is not open and visible, and so instead of employing shifting moral groupings of character Trollope uses a strict surface pattern in order to provoke our reading of the underlying myopia. The sharp contrast that he makes between the high-minded Scroopes and the equivocal Mrs O'Hara and her devious priest, with their limited political horizons, masks the covert parallel which only slowly emerges; for in this novel self-interest takes on many guises and is a morally levelling factor. The stark contrast between the driving forces of the action, the wild, amoral Mrs O'Hara and the decorous, religious Lady Scroope, who engage in a tenacious struggle to effectively limit Neville's will, is rendered deeply ironic by their clear moral identification. Like Mrs O'Hara's absurd pride in her daughter's blood, which makes Neville an attractive victim, Lady Scroope's fanatical commitment to the claims of birth renders her prevention of a match between the heir and the Irish peasant girl imperative, and the scene in which Mrs O'Hara confronts Neville with the result of her scheming finds its parallel in Lady Scroope's sober exhortation to him to place his obligation to Scroope before his immediate duty to the wronged girl. Similarly, the overt distinction between the rivals Sophia Mellerby and Kate O'Hara masks their basic commitment to the same moral category, for both employ sexual politics to feed their wills. And the other pair of would-be rivals, Fred Neville and his brother Jack, are also explicitly contrasted and covertly compared. The man of reason makes a striking contrast with the man of feeling, who naïvely believes that 'to be free to choose for himself in all things, was the highest privilege of man' (I, 62–3). Jack, who is the spokesman for Scroope, makes the intellectual statement which summarizes the expediency of the Scroope ethos and the deterministic philosophy which informs the world of the novel, when he remarks that '[c]ircumstances are stronger than predilections' (I, 90). However, in chasing Sophia Mellerby's fortune in order to redeem his position as a younger brother, Jack Neville is in secret competition with the Scroope world. And his cynical manipulation of circumstance, like his brother's thoughtless pursuit of his predilections, is rooted in egoism and hedged around with equivocation, as are all human actions in this novel.

The pattern of *An Eye for An Eye* is further developed by Trollope's use of the paired scene. Each section of the novel contains reciprocal scenes of temptation and debate. The subtle presence of Lady Scroope in the apparently private and random encounter between Sophia Mellerby and Fred Neville at Scroope, surrounded by ancestral portraits reminding him emblematically of his duty, is balanced by the sexually charged scene with Kate O'Hara on the Irish coast, in which her mother's hand is crudely in evidence. At Ardkill Cottage Neville is devoted to Kate, but at Scroope Manor he realizes her lack of fitness to be a countess and he takes refuge in fantastic equivocal schemes which would allow the couple to spend their married life on board a yacht. And while his movement between England and Ireland makes a physical correlative for his vacillating nature, the careful pattern which these scenes make also serves to give a roundness to his character which the other figures lack. We can watch the fluid movement of his consciousness crystallizing to points of decision and then dissolving again under the pressure of circumstance.

In *An Eye for An Eye* Trollope also articulates time in a special way by evoking vistas of the past, because time governs the tragedy. A brief flashback judiciously intercalated into the narrative reveals that the reclusive Earl's involvement with his heir's prospective marriage is, after all, deeply egotistical; for his son, the previous heir, broke the old man's heart by rejecting his choice of a bride and marrying instead a French prostitute.

And similarly, we learn of Mrs O'Hara's wretched marriage to a well-born rake and his subsequent abandonment of both her and her child. Trollope carefully places these revelations early in the novel so that by the end of its opening section they make a strong ironic parallel. Just as for Earl and Lady Scroope Neville's possible marriage to a low-born, penniless, foreign Catholic girl threatens a tragic repetition of the past, so too for Mrs O'Hara the fledgling lord's imminent desertion of her pregnant daughter foreshadows a renewal of her own past grief and guilt. Neville's butterfly romance is thus placed in a profoundly ironic perspective by these juxtaposed histories of other people's past choices which are now working on him with dedicated intensity. In truth his freedom is more limited than any one of the characters knows and Jack Neville's earlier statement is invested with redoubled ironic force as others' lives impinge on Fred Neville's actions with cumulative and tragic effect.

Trollope intensifies the psychological pressure placed on Neville and gives an added sense of inevitability to the development of the plot by allowing him no scenes into which to escape. And an important measure of temporal unity also contributes to this effect, for the action spans Neville's one year of freedom with his regiment before he settles down to his domestic duties. This constitutes the limited period within which Mrs O'Hara must contrive to secure him for her daughter and which Lady Scroope has to thwart her. The rhythm of this crisis is mirrored in the novel's structure. The ensnaring of Neville, which occupies the long opening section, takes from October until March; the rapid piling up of events in the central section occurs during the next three months; while the resolution of the conflict, during which time suddenly becomes crowded and urgent, takes a mere three days in midsummer. But it is Fred Neville's character, his continual denial of the very existence of a crisis, that governs the ironic form of *An Eye for An Eye* and Trollope therefore also employs time for its shock value. The decisive suddenness of the Earl's death and Neville's easy assumption of his new role leads inevitably to his murder. Clearly chance rules with a fine impartiality over the world of the novel and is part of its meaning. While the particularity of Neville's character is destiny, the casual juxtaposition of the lives of the Scroopes and the O'Haras is chance. And the accident of Neville's interposition at the heart of this conflict of similar but separate destinies, which he is utterly unfitted to resolve, generates a powerful sense of the operation of fate in human lives. The mimetic adequacy and tragic power of *An Eye for An Eye* depends, not on Trollope's presentation of the 'Ideal' behind the 'Real' as in *Nina Balatka*, but on his ability to convey a sense of strictly conditional freedom.

Coincidence, then, forms an important part of the novel's structure and takes its place in the pattern of foreshadowing which focuses our attention on the final scene of Fred Neville's murder. This is first anticipated in the early flashback by which we learn of Mrs O'Hara's own desertion, her social isolation, her physical power, her incipient madness and her strange obsession with the claims of blood (I, 38–9). Our expectations are heightened by the horror with which she foresees her own fate befalling her daughter and her determination to avenge it (I, 44, 47); by the violence she offers her gloating husband when he returns, and by Neville's own premonitions when he leaves Scroope and as he nears the Irish cliffs. Trollope thus renders Neville's death necessary both in dramatic and in psychological terms. By ruining her daughter's life as well as her own, Mrs O'Hara has incurred a double guilt, and in thrusting Fred Neville from the Heights of Moher she exacts a double vengeance. The phrase 'an eye for an eye', which she repeats exultantly in the asylum, thus possesses an obscure but profoundly personal significance and encapsulates at the same time Trollope's tragic vision of human destiny. But his sense of the appropriate dramatic form, of closure and completion, is perhaps most in evidence in the final scene. The place of Neville's misdeed becomes the arena for his great retribution and the focal point of his illusion of freedom is abruptly transformed into the place of his death. The ironic effect of this almost casual revolution of fortune's wheel is completed in the temporal scheme of the novel, for his year of freedom in Ireland is ended and it is once again midsummer. Although the character of

Neville, a man unable to choose until the possibility of making a true choice has long passed, is central to the novel, the psychology of the two women who dramatize the terms of his choice so urgently is also important. And Trollope finally draws the parallel between the insane Mrs O'Hara and the penitent Lady Scroope, locked away in the asylum and the chapel of the manor house, to emphasize their collective guilt and to amplify the tyranny of the imprisoning claims of the past. It is a pattern which stresses Trollope's profound awareness of the strange, ironic contingency of human life and in common with his other experimental novels it also summarizes his bleakly tragic, 'un-Trollopian' vision.

IV
THE RHETORICAL DESIGN

The Rhetoric of *Orley Farm*

MID-VICTORIAN critics distinguished between the dramatic novel, which they praised for its unity, autonomy and realism, and the novel that was dominated by the author's voice, which they felt to be lax and inartistic. Reviewers displayed a marked preference for 'showing' rather than 'telling' and those novels which were constructed on the basis of 'scene' instead of 'summary' received loud and often undiscriminating praise.[1] As Trollope was the rising star among the novelists at this period, it was natural that his methods should become the focus of this particular debate and several reviewers readily identified in his novels what they considered to be his abuse of the author's voice. The *Saturday Review*, for instance, was critical of his procedure in *The Small House at Allington* because: 'Mr Trollope . . . sets a very bad example to other novelists in the frequency with which he has recourse to the petty trick of passing a judgment on his own fictitious personages as he goes along, in order that the story may thus seem to have an existence independent of its teller, and to form a subject on which he can speculate as on something outside himself'.[2] Henry James on the other hand, who believed that the novel should have the same kind of validity as history, complained that Trollope destroyed this autonomy by taking delight 'in reminding the reader that the story he was telling was only, after all, a make-believe'.[3] This critical confusion about the function of Trollope's narrative voice mirrors the Victorian critics' general

89

uncertainty as to whether the novel should be viewed primarily as art or as history. And this debate has continued for so long in Trollope criticism precisely because Trollope's rhetoric mediates continually between life as something to be lived and fiction as something that is made.[4]

Essentially, both Henry James and the *Saturday Review* critic are complaining that Trollope's method puts the reader in a false position. I believe, however, that the creation of a stable relation between the author, his reader and the world of his fiction is a fundamental aspect of Trollope's rhetoric. Indeed, he had enunciated his conception of this relation as early as *Barchester Towers*, in Chapter XV :

> Our doctrine is, that the author and the reader should move along together in full confidence with each other. Let the personages of the drama undergo ever so complete a comedy of errors among themselves, but let the spectator never mistake the Syracusan for the Ephesian; otherwise he is one of the dupes, and the part of a dupe is never dignified. (p. 130).

Trollope never allows his reader to become his dupe, but in spite of this assertion (which is itself of course part of his rhetorical procedure in *Barchester Towers*) and Henry James's confidence that Trollope 'never juggled with the sympathies or the credulity of his reader',[5] his narrative voice does continually manipulate the reader's response. At the beginning of *Orley Farm*, for instance, it achieves several effects which depend on establishing a firm relation with the reader. 'It is not true', Trollope tells us in his opening sentence, 'that a rose by any other name will smell as sweet. Were it true, I should call this story "The Great Orley Farm Case". But who would ask for the ninth number of a serial work burthened with so very uncouth an appellation?' (I, 1). Trollope's whimsical revelation of the nature of his story and his bluff admission of a certain professional sharpness function to bind the reader to him, but this 'little slap at credulity', as Henry James called this use of Trollope's authorial tone,[6] also enforces from the beginning the reader's clear sense of the novel as fiction rather than history. And yet within a few sentences the narrative voice begins to establish the autonomy of the novel's world. Trollope ceases to talk of 'this book of mine' and discusses as if they were historical truth those 'legal questions which made a considerable stir in our courts of law' (I, 1). The reader quickly learns, therefore, that Trollope's fiction inhabits the interface between art and life and that his narrator frequently mediates between both.

But Trollope's almost imperceptible shift from fiction to fact is most important in creating the novel's illusion of a self-contained world, and throughout the novel the narrative voice is continually active in building up the reader's sense of his entering a unified world with its own set of rules which works just like real Victorian life, in order that he may participate fully in the fiction offered for his sympathy and judgement without the necessity to keep referring outside the novel to his own experience. Trollope's narrator builds into this world a system of detailed correspondences which occur, for example, in the sphere of work, which makes up such a large area of *Orley Farm*. Its legal world is given solidity as we learn that barristers come into their prime in their fifties instead of in their forties like other professional men, that it is not quite the thing for a barrister to wait upon an attorney, or that there is as complex an etiquette among commercial travellers as among lawyers; we discover that there is a strict hierarchical order among housemaids, chambermaids and cooks; and we learn too about the financial prospects of chemists' assistants in London.[7] And Trollope's capacity to mediate between his reader's world and his fictionalized world also depends upon his creation of shared conventional values. His narrator praises public schools, inveighs against public examinations and extols domestic contentment; and he does this so successfully that the critic for the *National Review* called his review of *Orley Farm*, 'Trollope as the voice of the English middle class'. But Trollope also invests his world with a psychological density by means of generalized observations that the reader can recognize. There are the shy, awkward men like John Kenneby who nurse an intense inner life; there is the truth that 'there is nothing perhaps so generally consoling to a man as a well-established grievance' (I, 81), and there are glimpses into the psychology of officialdom: 'To the police-

91

man's mind every man not a policeman is a guilty being, and the attorneys perhaps share something of this feeling' (II, 207).

Trollope's ability to secure the reader's commitment to a realistic world seemingly contiguous with his own is essential to the creation of a stable relation between the author, the reader and the fiction. And this effect of stability is fundamental to Trollope's moral rhetoric which seeks to dislocate his reader's secure, conventional ethical response without making a complete rupture with the author or his fictional world. Trollope never quite dupes his reader, nor does he ever quite remove the overwhelming impression in the reader's mind that he has entered an autonomous, realistic world. But he does create the important effect of a profound and continuous tension between art and life, because in spite of his elaborate pretence that the novel is history, he also constantly draws attention to its patent artifice and nowhere more obviously than when he introduces Lady Mason to the reader at the commencement of *Orley Farm* :

I trust that it is already perceived by all persistent novel readers that very much of the interest of this tale will be centred in the person of Lady Mason. Such educated persons, however, will probably be aware that she is not intended to be the heroine. The heroine, so called, must by a certain fixed law be young and marriageable. Some such heroine in some future number shall be forthcoming, with as much of the heroic about her as may be found convenient; but for the present let it be understood that the person and character of Lady Mason is as important to us as can be those of any young lady, let her be ever so gracious or ever so beautiful. (I, 12–13).

Here Trollope reminds us forcefully of the conventionality of art and of those laws of fiction which we have erected to minister to our egotistical desires : our need of youthful heroines like Madeline Staveley, whom he has promised to introduce, or marriages like that between Madeline Staveley and Felix Graham at the conclusion of the novel, or a simple system of reward and punishment. In drawing attention to this pattern of wish-fulfilment in fiction, Trollope is undermining his reader's moral security, challenging his sense of the completeness and meaning which fiction offers and reminding him at the same time of the fluidity and insecurity of life. But this narrative address also functions as a clear reading direction for Trollope does in fact find much that is admirable and even heroic in the lovely woman who boldly forged her husband's will, courageously survives two trials and finally stands exonerated. And by thus disrupting the novel's conventional morality, Trollope complicates our response both to fiction and to life. The form of the novel is thus extended and made more flexible and realistic as its moral categories and conventional patterns are probed and questioned.

Clearly Trollope's subtle rhetoric serves his moral vision. Like the majority of mid-Victorian critics, who were in no doubt that the highest art should convey moral lessons,[8] he felt that novels had taken the place of sermons,[9] and in his *Autobiography* he declares himself unequivocally a moralist.[10] The corollary, of course, as Trollope well understood, is that 'the novelist, if he have a conscience . . . must have his own system of ethics'.[11] Ruth apRoberts has described Trollope's moral position as so advanced as to be defined as 'Situation Ethics',[12] and certainly in *Orley Farm* his sustained defence of Lady Mason, who successfully defies all moral, legal and fictional codes, seems to fit her analysis of Trollope's strenuous exercise of moral pragmatism. For instance, in that intense scene of Lady Mason's confession of guilt to Sir Peregrine Orme, where Trollope charts the conflict between her necessary moral empiricism and his moral absolutism, the situation clearly calls for the conventional reader's condemnation. However, we have been already made aware that she possesses the instincts of a lady and that her confession is wrung from her by a generous love. And moments of moral sensitivity and inner torment like these suddenly evade the straightjacket of fictional convention and register in the reader a profound moral shock. For Trollope has forced us to identify with a remarkable character in an extraordinary moral situation; has required us in effect to test our own system of values, and has made us uncomfortably aware of the simplified demands we habitually make both upon art and upon life.

And yet I do not wholeheartedly agree with Ruth apRoberts

that Trollope is a moral relativist simply. In spite of all his attacks on the kinds of novel conventions that demand among other things a nemesis,[13] I believe that Trollope, like George Eliot, has a strong sense of a natural justice at work in the world. But its mode of operation takes no account either of traditional fictional or Victorian ethical conventions; it rather works within and through character and produces the self-torture of isolated individuals like Louis Trevelyan, Julia Brabazon or Lady Mason. There is a working out of reward and punishment in *Orley Farm*, but the reader finds it at the same time both reassuring and disconcerting, because it affirms the strength of moral impulses in human lives, yet it bypasses the simple conventional patterns of the novel and overturns social mechanisms.

Trollope's rhetoric clearly revolts from didacticism – from the garrulous intimacy that he objects to in the Thackerayan narrator, for instance.[14] As he remarks in a letter to Kate Field about the manuscript of her novel: 'Your reader should not be made to think that *you* are trying to teach or to preach, or to convince. Teach, and preach, and convince if you can; – but first learn the art of doing so without seeming to do it.'[15] For Trollope, as I have been suggesting, this art eschews equally both narrative sermonizing and the cruder patterns of wish-fulfilment. The key to our understanding of Trollope's moral rhetoric resides in the great importance he attached to his relation with his reader and in the absolutely central place that character holds in his art. His major figures are neither wholly good nor wholly bad, but 'mixed' and as such they demand both our sympathy and our judgement. We are led to feel compassion for villains like George Vavasor, Ferdinand Lopez and even Augustus Melmotte, and we are also made alive to the weaknesses of worthy people like Mr Crawley, Mark Roberts, Harry Clavering or Lady Mason. In my view, what moulds Trollope's flexible relation between the author, his characters and his reader, and is at the same time fluid enough to mediate between fictional pattern and moral truth, is a complex rhetoric of sympathy and judgement.

One of the more interesting and surprising aspects of Trollope's rhetorical art is the way it developed out of the mid-Victorian debate about the form and function of the novel.

94

A prominent participant in this discussion was Trollope's friend, the novelist and student of fiction, Edward Bulwer-Lytton, who was an advocate of the dramatic in fiction but who also argued for a freer form for the novel. One of his particular interests was the relation between the author and the reader and in 1860 and 1861, when Trollope was engaged in writing *Orley Farm*, Bulwer-Lytton was working on a series of articles, some of which dealt with this subject, later to be published in *Blackwood's Edinburgh Magazine* under the title 'Caxtoniana'.[16] It is probable that Bulwer-Lytton discussed his ideas with Trollope, but in any case there is a striking similarity between their views. Like Trollope, Bulwer-Lytton is suspicious of novels which appeal only to the intellectual reader and he maintains that their characters must embody compelling emotions with which a miscellaneous audience can establish sympathy.[17] In his lecture, 'On English Prose Fiction', Trollope puts it this way:

It all lies in that. No novel is anything, for purposes either of tragedy or of comedy, unless the reader can sympathise with the characters whose names he finds upon the page . . . Truth let there be; — truth of description, truth of character, human truth as to men and women.[18]

Bulwer-Lytton and Trollope also agree that the reader can only share the author's knowledge of his characters if their creator has first been sympathetically involved in their lives. In his *Autobiography* Trollope gives us his well-known description of this process of identification:

[the novelist] desires to make his readers so intimately acquainted with his characters that the creations of his brain should be to them speaking, moving, living, human creatures. This he can never do unless he know those fictitious personages himself, and he can never know them well unless he can live with them in the full reality of established intimacy.[19]

But the rhetorical process is more complex than this, for the author's moral intellect is also at work judging his characters. This is where the emphasis falls in Bulwer-Lytton's early essay, 'On Art in Fiction',[20] and Trollope elaborates his position in his *Autobiography*:

[the author] must argue with [his characters], quarrel with them, forgive them, and even submit to them. He must know of them whether they be cold-blooded or passionate, whether true or false, and how far true, and how far false. The depth and the breadth, and the narrowness and the shallowness of each should be clear to him.[21]

What Bulwer-Lytton and Trollope are outlining is a creative paradox, an imaginative co-operation between sympathy and judgement, since the author's uncompromising critical intellect should be as strong as his moral identification. And the reader, in making this kind of moral scrutiny, needs to be distanced from the characters, an effect which is best achieved by the use of irony; for while sympathy serves to suspend the reader's judgement, irony serves to sharpen it. It is this continual interplay between sympathy and irony that forms the basis of Trollope's moral rhetoric in *Orley Farm* and it clearly is a method flexible enough to include both 'scene' and 'summary', to mediate between the conventions of the novel and the evolution of natural justice which depends on much subtler relations between character and form, and to articulate connections between the autonomous social world of the novel and the moral situation of the tormented woman isolated at its centre.

Although it was admired by George Eliot and Trollope himself thought it one of his best novels, in recent times *Orley Farm* has been frequently misread. Bradford Booth believes that it is artistry *manqué*,[22] Robert M. Adams calls it a 'patchwork affair' which 'does not prove its moral as novels must',[23] while Robert M. Polhemus's view of Lady Mason as a 'deeply flawed woman' throws his interpretation of the novel off balance.[24] These misreadings have occurred, I think, because critics have tended to ignore the novel's subtle rhetoric. In my view *Orley Farm* owes a great deal to Bulwer-Lytton's theory. It would be difficult to exaggerate how thoroughly Trollope's creation of a rhetorical design, shaped by the complex interplay of sympathy with irony, informs the novel at all levels. And this design is perfectly adjusted to the novel's central unifying concern, the complex nature of moral judgement. For its main issue of how to judge the enigmatic Lady Mason, whose trial forms the catalyst for Trollope's sardonic vision, engages all the major

characters and the reader is immediately involved in the process. As his mock apology later in the novel suggests, Trollope
regards Lady Mason not merely as a criminal, but also as a
social victim and as a good and even heroic woman. At the
same time he also alerts the reader to the process that lies at
the heart of the novel's rhetorical pattern:

> I may, perhaps be thought to owe an apology to my readers in that I
> have asked their sympathy for a woman who had so sinned as to have
> placed her beyond the general sympathy of the world at large. . . . But
> as I have told her story that sympathy has grown upon myself till I
> have learned to forgive her, and to feel that I too could have regarded
> her as a friend. (II, 404).

Beneath this disarmingly simple defence of Lady Mason lurks
the ironic assertion that *Orley Farm* possesses a rhetoric designed
to challenge the Victorian reader's blind allegiance to the conventional morality of the nineteenth-century novel. But more
importantly, *Orley Farm* is one of Trollope's most sustained
assaults on the moral code of the Victorian middle classes, for
which he felt such a high price was being paid in human misery.
And in this novel two distinct but fundamental aspects of the
code are inseparably entangled: the Victorians' profound belief
in the infallibility of the law as the custodian of public morality
and in the sanctity of womanhood as the regulator of moral
conduct in the home. Trollope employs Lady Mason's guilt,
which threatens both of these myths and automatically incurs
punitive responses, to demonstrate how the impossibly high
ideals which they enshrine serve to display society's unhealthy
contempt for human frailty. What is more, the inflexibility of
this absolutist morality, which masks its extreme fragility,
resting as it does on a consensus of will, undermines the strength
of the private conscience and makes responsible judgements
difficult, if not impossible.

The intensely dramatic scene of Lady Mason's confession,
which occurs midway through the novel, is designed to carry a
heavy rhetorical burden and its multiple perspectives of sympathy and irony suggest the true complexity of moral scrutiny.[25] A sympathetic effect is created by the profound realism

of its psychological undercurrents. Just as, having been sold as bankrupt stock on the marriage market by her ruined parents and cheated by her avaricious husband Sir Joseph Mason, Lady Mason employs his commercial ethic to defeat him, so in relation to another father-figure, her potential husband Sir Peregrine Orme, she sacrificially adopts his straight-jacket morality to save him from public disgrace. But she is not a moral chameleon. Her powerful response to both base meanness and high-minded generosity is in each case a splendid assertion of the fundamental empiricism of the personal conscience in human relations. However, in the shocked reactions of the aging baronet Trollope strikingly reveals two powerful yet disparate elements of neo-Calvinism at work in the Victorian world. A fixed code cannot be reconciled with the equally strong claim of the sanctity of the private conscience and our sympathy for Lady Mason is accompanied by an ironic distancing in judgement on Sir Peregrine Orme, who invokes blinkered absolutist notions of repentance and restitution. The subtle, ironic movement of the scene makes his social reflex the surrogate for the average reader's moral response to her sensational crime and flagrant breach of feminine mythology, while at the same time he is encouraged to identify with the warm response of Sir Peregrine's daughter-in-law, Mrs Orme. Although she is the main representative of saintly Victorian womanhood in the novel, Mrs Orme makes a mature, compassionate assessment of Lady Mason's unique human situation which involves a moral relativism that ironically runs counter to the canons of public respectability, and which is vindicated as the scene illumines Lady Mason's motives and foreshadows her agonizing retribution.

Lady Mason's role as a social victim is the long-delayed but inescapable effect of her passion for equity and her cheating of the law to obtain it. Because she never thought of her action in forging her husband's monstrously unfair will as anything but just and has never considered it from the point of view of social ethics, the revelation of Sir Peregrine's moral horror is a traumatic experience. Paradoxically, Trollope's concern to secure our balanced moral judgement means that he is never entirely neutral or objective and Lady Mason's prostration in the fireless room, huddled in a shawl, suffering the chill of moral exclusion, makes a covert though powerful appeal as an emblem of her state of mind. It works in conjunction with the complex flow of the reader's sympathy and emotion: admiration for her self-sacrifice, fear as she contemplates the future and an element of physical suffering that sharpens our response to her mental anguish, which is effectively evoked through Mrs Orme's instinctive gesture of human warmth and approval in lighting the fire and ministering to her immediate needs.

Mrs Orme's indefinitely deferred judgement of Lady Mason marks her as the chief spokesman for Trollope's rhetoric of sympathy and this is balanced by Felix Graham's fitful role as ironist. By this means Trollope effectively avoids intrusive moralizing, but he is careful that neither spokesman fully represents his own moral vision. The fledgling attorney is obsessed with arriving at an abstract legal judgement of Lady Mason's case, while Mrs Orme is absorbed by the human need. One is concerned with justice, the other with equity. However, their main function is to present, from opposite points of view, cogent reasons why the reader must eschew simple, definitive moral judgements. Felix Graham's ultra-idealistic posture serves to emphasize that it is no good looking to the law for equity in human affairs. Its double standards are most clearly in evidence at the emblematically futile legal congress in Birmingham, the ironic centre of society's purely commercial values. Graham's sympathy for the visionary speaker Von Bauhr exposes the gulf which exists between the heady pretensions which the congress enshrines and the rooted cynicism of its participating lawyers; for Mr Chaffanbrass's sneers form an appropriate commentary on the frantic attempts of Lady Mason's lawyer, Mr Furnival, to get the case against his client quietly dropped. And in private life the moral chaos of the legal system is aptly summarized in a parallel domestic scene by Judge Staveley's participation in the emblematic fumbling chase of blind man's buff during the Christmas celebrations at Noningsby, where the human face of the law and also its fallibility are exposed: ' "Justice is blind," said Graham. "Why should a judge be ashamed to follow the example of his own goddess?" ' (I, 223). Graham, of course, confuses justice with equity because his faith in the law is divorced from his contempt for the system, but like all the main characters in attacking one double standard he is trapped by another, for his sweeping condemnation of Lady Mason and her lawyers, which makes a submerged parallel with the harsh judgement of her made earlier by Sir Peregrine Orme, is only partly directed at the legal situation. As his theoretical attempt to train a wife implies, what he really loathes is Lady Mason's breaking of a deeply-cherished myth. His idealism is ultimately rooted in egoism and it is in this context that the irony of Judge Staveley's fatherly reprimand: ' "Graham, my dear fellow, judge not that you be not judged" ' (II, 122), which lies quietly at the heart of the novel's rhetoric, cuts through these moral ambiguities and includes the reader within its frame of reference.

Trollope's placing of his central moral statement midway through the novel marks a shift in its rhetorical weight. As Graham's role as spokesman is undercut by the dichotomy between his public posture and his private life, so Trollope stresses the wholeness and integrity of Mrs Orme's point of view. Just as he employs the interpolation from Molière's *L'École des Femmes* to discredit Graham as the spokesman for idealism in the novel, so in the moral relation between Lady Mason and her Good Angel, Mrs Orme, he draws on elements of Marlowe's *Doctor Faustus*.[26] As Mrs Orme is suddenly thrust from her sheltered life into the public arena of Lady Mason's trial she is most strongly contrasted with Felix Graham, whose high-mindedness crumbles into petulant frustration at the inequity of the legal process, while Mrs Orme, in spite of her knowledge of the woman's guilt, courageously supports the wretched Lady Mason. Trollope's rhetoric of sympathy is at work in the intense moral relation between the two women which serves to deepen our understanding of Lady Mason as the second trial duplicates the first. The present agony is felt the more keenly as the past is more fully revealed. A widow, with a son Lucius Mason's age, Mrs Orme alone is competent to judge the nature of Lady Mason's temptation, the desperation of her desire to preserve her innocent son's good name and the quest for equity which makes victory at the second trial a moral as well as a psycho-logical imperative. And her refusal to do so gains a special signifi-cance. She recognizes the fundamental incompatibility of rigid public ethics and the fluid inner life of personal conscience, and unlike the idealists, Sir Peregrine Orme and Felix Graham, she rejects the static view of human character that an inflexible moral system implies; for she has observed how twenty years of lonely anguish suffered on behalf of her penniless son and her scrupulous act of conscience to protect Sir Peregrine Orme have ennobled Lady Mason. She not only sympathizes, but she is morally in her debt.

The relation between the novel's social realism, its treatment of character and its rhetorical design is partly articulated by Trollope's use of masks. As Lady Mason's story demonstrates, character may not simply be related to the rhetorical structure, but may in a meaningful sense be that structure, for the inevit-able unfolding of her story is also the progressive revelation of her character. The emergence of Lady Mason's inner nature develops the novel's central contrast between public and private judgement as Trollope exploits the ironic gap which exists be-tween her public mask and her private face. Her mask is un-willingly assumed and worn with sorrow, and its unpeeling in the course of the novel is a sympathetic as well as an ironic process. Pity for her is most strongly felt immediately before she goes to the court, in a scene charged with high irony when she breaks down before her son's priggish resentment at her reticence, but dare not let him learn the cause of her distress. Her subsequent movement from the private to the public ordeal elicits admiration for her sheer power of will as she carefully restores for the trial the impenetrably composed façade that she had first assumed for the same occasion twenty years before. And inside the courtroom this mask allows Trollope to explore the relation between the inward and the social worlds in greater depth. The main irony which the public mask reveals is that, despite the effective myth, public judgement, unlike the law, bears no relation to the rigid yet fragile bourgeois morality it is supposed to represent, but is a crude and frighteningly casual process. Public faces are intended to deceive and the packed

courtroom at first believes Lady Mason innocent. For the specta-
tors, however, the operation of the law is simply diverting
theatre and when the evidence points plainly to her guilt they
merely alter their mode of illusion and applaud her coolness for
the accomplished mask of a heroine forger. For the larger world
there is no double standard because there exists no standard
at all.

This is the world of Moulder, the commercial traveller, whose
ethics dominate the novel. And Trollope's ironic method includes the use of Moulder as his temporary spokesman, who
assumes a position which is being attacked by the author (II,
215–17). The victim and his point of view are allowed to take
over completely and his words condemn him utterly as Trollope employs the device of the mask and the accompanying
shock in a deadly form. His method is a kind of *reductio ad
absurdum*. The commercial code underpinning the law (which
we have already witnessed in the confrontation between
Moulder and the attorney Dockwrath at the Bull Inn, Leeds)
which Sir Peregrine cannot bring himself to believe and which
Felix Graham deplores, is frankly applauded by Moulder. He
enjoys the sale of truth and stories of the guilty escaping justice
by feeing sharp lawyers, and will wager ten pounds on Lady
Mason's acquittal. And the intimidation of honest witnesses
also appeals to his bullying nature, but it is the sovereign impartiality of wealth that calls forth his hyperbole: ' "Unfair!"
said Moulder. "It's the fairest thing that is. It's the bulwark
of the British Constitution" ' (II, 216).

It is from this threateningly amoral world of the masses, of
frank hedonists like Moulder and his fellow commercial traveller, Kantwise, 'pigs out of the sty of Epicurus' (I, 246) as Trollope calls them, that the middle classes retreat into defensively
rigid codes. But as Trollope shows so clearly, these unattain-
ably high standards result in people erecting complex façades
to evade the constant moral scrutiny of daily life. Worn as a
matter of habit they are also a means of avoiding claims on one's
humanity. This is what links men as different as the nostalgically
conservative Sir Peregrine Orme and the abrasively radical
Felix Graham. Their human responses freeze into clumsy and

inappropriate moral postures. And in *Orley Farm* these masks are also emblematic of double standards of behaviour and judgement. Sir Peregrine Orme and Felix Graham also share a blind faith in the law which means that at first they are easily deceived about Lady Mason. To the crafty lawyers, however, who know that the verdict of the courts represents justice rather than equity and for whom humanity's façades are their stock in trade, her guilt is transparently obvious. Yet they too are absolved from making a responsible judgement, not by their beliefs, but by their professional roles. Legal etiquette forbids that they mention her guilt and the system of advocacy requires that they conceal it. Ironically however, while as lawyers they uphold public morality, when their masks slip a little they are revealed as men who are bored by the dull proprieties of Victorian society and it is as men, rather than as lawyers, that their interest and sympathy are aroused by the beautiful woman's secret guilt.

The assumption of masks baffles the achievement of justice and equity and it also stultifies human intercourse. More importantly, however, as the precise regulation of conduct puts an intolerable strain on the individual personality and the mask is increasingly used to evade self-scrutiny, it threatens the inward life. The ironic shock of recognition that in Joseph Mason, Lady Mason's persecutor, mask and face have become identical, distances us in judgement on his horrifying egoism. Ostensibly his mindless rigidity of outlook simply reflects the impersonal law of equity which rules his life and to which he clings long after it has become absurd and destructive. But at a deeper level this constitutes a complex façade employed to cover his flight from self-judgement. His paranoiac concern with equity, which he confuses with justice, is really an obscure source of self-justification: 'Justice, outraged justice, was his theme. Whom had he ever robbed? To whom had he not paid all that was owing? "All that have I done from my youth upwards." Such were his thoughts of himself' (II, 239). Clearly this mask has a different function and value from Lady Mason's and the moral contrast between the two antagonists is brought out by Mason's own 'trial'. It occurs in a fascinating moment, made powerful by the complex interplay of sympathy with irony, when Lady Mason enters the courtroom and confronts her accuser : 'As she thus looked her gaze fell on one face that she had not seen for years, and their eyes met. It was the face of Joseph Mason of Groby, who sat opposite to her; and as she looked at him her own countenance did not quail for a moment. Her own countenance did not quail; but his eyes fell gradually down, and when he raised them again she had averted her face' (II, 248). This moment encapsulates their shared experience of the past, confirms Lady Mason's moral superiority and secures our moral commitment to her at her moment of most intense crisis. At the same time it also ironically foreshadows the function of the law in achieving equity, for Mason is soon to be trapped by his obsession. The passion for justice which he has projected onto the law renders him the victim of its brutal and inefficient commercial system. He thus falls by the code he has lived by and this fleeting moment becomes emblematic of the way outraged natural justice brings about nemesis in the fulness of time.

This is an important aspect of the rhetorical design of *Orley Farm*, a novel which challenges our allegiance to the kind of simple morality enshrined in the traditional conventions of the novel, which encourages our acceptance of the need for moral relativism and yet which also includes a realistic vision of a natural moral order, firmly rooted in antecedent human experience, asserting itself through character and the fluctuating ironies of life. The conclusion of Lady Mason's trial reaches a point of moral equilibrium which embodies a synthesis of our contrary impulses to sympathize and to judge. And it is to this point that Trollope's elaborate, complex but subtle rhetoric has imperceptibly led us. Although her acquittal, which avoids the obvious injustice of a verdict in favour of the vicious Joseph Mason, corresponds to our sympathetic knowledge of her innate nobility, the trial also engineers her public shame and her retribution. The private principles of equity and moral empiricism are vindicated while the public myths of legal infallibility and feminine purity are preserved. In the larger development of the novel the growth of our sympathy for Lady Mason is balanced by Trollope's achievement of an aesthetic distance so that we can judge life's victims with critical detachment.

This depends on our awareness in *Orley Farm* of the quiet presence of the traditional tragic pattern of hubris (pride), hamartia (an error of judgement) and nemesis (divine retribution), governed by a natural moral law, which gives shape to Lady Mason's life and binds it firmly to the social world of the novel. It includes all the egoists within its scope and the precise form of their retribution has an ironic appropriateness. Trollope makes it clear that Lady Mason's excessive love for her unworthy son is a subtle form of egoism and that her passion for equity is tainted by pride in her vengeance on an unjust social order. And in reclaiming the land from Dockwrath when her son comes of age she re-enacts her original crime and sets in motion the train of events which leads inexorably to her second trial. It is not the crime, but her refusal to accept the second chance that life offers her to alter her moral direction, that brings upon her the very fate she has striven to avoid, the ruin and humiliation of her son. And similarly, Joseph Mason's scheming for vengeance under the cloak of justice achieves no more than simple equity in the return of the farm to him, which occurs independently of the legal process. His faith in the law, which appeared to enshrine his harsh ethical code, merely ensures his moral defeat. Its true function as the catalyst and preserver of popular illusion is demonstrated in Lady Mason's victory, and Joseph Mason is left nursing an insatiable obsession. For his step-brother Lucius the ready espousal of public values also brings about his private anguish. He too becomes the ironic victim of his own fantasies, because it is his conceit in his new role as a landowner that resurrects the old legal battle and his nemesis comes at the moment of his mother's shocking confession immediately after the trial, which humbles him in the very instant of his triumphant vindication. Even Sir Peregrine Orme is brought within the scope of retributive justice for, although Trollope overtly protects the reputation of the weak, he also insists on their share in the common guilt. Sympathy for the saddened old man is subtly balanced by one of the novel's most poignant ironies. When, after a great inner struggle, Sir Peregrine has courageously succeeded in revaluing the moral outlook of a whole lifetime and has broken free of the imprisoning attitudes of Victorian mythology, it is Mrs Orme, his paragon of womanhood, who strenuously invokes them afresh in resolutely opposing his marriage with Lady Mason. Her earlier presence in the courtroom at Lady Mason's side, a pairing emblematic of their shared moral convictions, really concealed a potent irony which Trollope permits to surface late in the novel with devastating rhetorical effect. In spite of her undoubtedly generous humanity, even Mrs Orme cannot reconcile the contrary demands of the neo-Calvinist ethic, the claims of the private conscience and those of public standards, when an issue touches her closely. But this in turn conceals a further irony. It is essentially a false dilemma employed to mask her true commitment because, while in preventing the match she is overtly defending the family's good name, in truth, like Lady Mason, she is really protecting the financial security and prospects of her son. Mrs Orme's ironic capitulation to the commercial ethic demonstrates, perhaps more than anything else in the novel, the destructive power of a rigid moral code and its corrupting function of cloaking squalid self-interest.

In many ways *Orley Farm* is Trollope's *Measure for Measure*, but especially so in the way it raises ethical problems rather than resolves them; and although it does not have a moral to 'prove' it is clearly the product of a profoundly moral intelligence. By means of its multiple perspectives of sympathy and irony Trollope reveals how contemporary social mythologies grow out of a contempt for humanity and he stresses the almost schizoid lives they compel people to live. Trollope emphasizes that moral scrutiny is a delicate and complex process and he urges a compassionate yet responsible judgement of human frailty. And he does so by probing our assumptions about the conventions of fiction, by unsettling our familiar search for pattern in both fiction and life and by showing us how the springs of natural justice are located in character. In *Orley Farm* rhetorical design, social realism and moral vision are artistically unified because, as Bulwer-Lytton and Trollope agree, they are intimately related in the act of imaginative creation.

Serial Design in *The Claverings*

Trollope is central to any study of the serial method of publication in the middle years of the Victorian period in the first place because of his great popularity with the mass of the reading public, since it was largely through the medium of the magazines that his contemporary reputation was made.[27] Thackeray, for instance, keenly felt his rival's success while *Framley Parsonage* was appearing in the *Cornhill* concurrently with the early chapters of his own novel *Philip*. As he wrote to Mrs Baxter: 'I think Trollope is much more popular with the Cornhill Magazine readers than I am: and I doubt whether I am not going down hill considerably in public favour.'[28] From the instant success of *Framley Parsonage* in 1860 until the end of Trollope's career almost all his novels first greeted the public in instalments, and a further reason for his significance as a serial writer was his willingness to experiment with the convention in response to the fluctuating pressures of the literary market. Many of his novels were serialized in magazines like the *Cornhill*, the *St Paul's Magazine*, *Blackwood's Magazine*, *Macmillan's Magazine*, or *Good Words*, and others, like *Orley Farm* or *Can You Forgive Her?*, appeared in monthly part issue, a system which was popular until the publication of *The Vicar of Bullhampton* in 1869 and 1870 marked its decline.[29] The shilling part issue had been popular with the novel-reading public by virtue of its cheapness and for its particular quality of suspense, but it was gradually killed by the shilling magazine which sprang up in the 1860s and which, as Trollope recognized, dealt the market a severe blow: 'The public finding that so much might be had for a shilling, in which a portion of one or more novels was always included, were unwilling to spend their money on the novel alone.'[30] Trollope and his publisher, George Smith, fought the incursion of the magazine by experimenting with thirty-two weekly issues at sixpence per issue. *The Last Chronicle of Barset* first appeared in this form and despite its conspicuous lack of success the experiment with sixpenny parts was repeated with *He Knew He Was Right*, this time with a different publisher, Virtue. The other form of publication which Trollope tried as a desperate response to the stiff competition from the magazines was the singular production of *The Prime Minister* in eight massive monthly issues, but it was by then an outmoded method of publication and this no doubt contributed to the novel's comparatively poor sales.[31]

Trollope's readiness to accommodate the literary market and his editors in his methods of publication is matched by his almost incredible precision in planning his serials. His work sheets reveal that he provided exactly forty-eight pages of manuscript for each instalment of *Framley Parsonage, The Small House at Allington* and *The Claverings*,[32] and although these first two novels were only partly written when publication was already in progress, his work sheets for *Framley Parsonage*, for instance, show careful preliminary planning with chapter titles decided beforehand and the serial divisions clearly marked. The result of this forethought is a manuscript remarkably free from revision and *The Claverings* displays a similar diligent preparation.[33] Trollope's obligation to achieve this kind of accuracy was determined not only by the length of the magazine page and the space allocated to the novel in its layout, but also by the specific nature of his contract with the editor. *The Claverings*, for example, which was written for the *Cornhill*, was to consist of 'sixteen numbers of 24 pages each'.[34] As a rule, Trollope did his utmost to oblige his publishers in the matter of serial instalments, and the serial once planned admitted of little alteration. But he was also very much concerned with the question of balance and continuity in the narrative, and with the equalizing of tensions and ironies. Thus his response in 1863 to a request from Edward Chapman for last-minute revisions was terse and insistent: 'I can not make it shorter than it should be, in order that it might suit the periodical',[35] and he concludes a letter to Arthur Locker in 1881 about the difficulties encountered in serializing *Marion Fay* on a note of testy pride: 'No writer ever made work come easier to the editor of a Periodical than do I'.[36]

However, the fundamental importance of Trollope's art as a serial novelist lies, I think, in his extraordinary attention to the way his novels were presented to the reader, and he had very firm views about the pernicious effect of the convention of serial publication when he came to write *Framley Parsonage*: 'I had felt that the rushing mode of publication to which the system of serial stories had given rise, and by which small parts as they were written were sent hot to the press, was injurious to the work done.'[37] He knew that his friend Thackeray scrambled frantically from one instalment to the next, alternating between lethargy and panic, and this method was forced on Trollope himself when Thackeray wanted *Framley Parsonage* in a hurry for the *Cornhill*. However, as Trollope makes abundantly clear in his *Autobiography*, he did not commence writing the novel until the development of its plot was firmly fixed in his imagination, and his comments on the dangers inherent in the serial mode of publication underline his artistic sense of the novel as a complex unity which he refused to allow the regular and mechanical demands of the instalment to impair:

It had already been a principle with me in my art, that no part of a novel should be published till the entire story was completed. I knew, from what I read from month to month, that this hurried publication of incompleted work was frequently, I might perhaps say always, adopted by the leading novelists of the day . . . I had not yet entered upon the system of publishing novels in parts, and therefore had never been tempted. But I was aware that an artist should keep in his hand the power of fitting the beginning of his work to the end.[38]

The convention was also suspect, in Trollope's view, because of its seductive ease of production which led to idleness,[39] and he considered that this is what mars the form of Thackeray's fiction, for he finds *Vanity Fair* 'vague and wandering, clearly commenced without any idea of an ending',[40] while in *Pendennis* 'You feel that each morsel as you read it is a detached bit, and that it has all been written in detachments'.[41]

In spite of Trollope's clear artistic intentions *Framley Parsonage*, which constituted his serial baptism, is also episodic, as the critic for the *Westminster Review* noted: 'The habit of writing a story in periodical instalments is almost always fatal to that coherence and proportion without which no work can lay claim to any really artistic merit. The consequence of this mode of publication is that "Framley Parsonage" is rather a series of anecdotes than a well-knit tale.'[42] However, after the resounding success of *Framley Parsonage* George Smith naturally wanted another novel from Trollope and his next contribution for the *Cornhill*, other than the stopgap *Brown, Jones and Robinson*, was *The Small House at Allington* which, in spite of its almost equal rapidity of production, displays more care both in the design of the novel and in the construction of the serial part. Trollope deliberately rounds off each instalment so that the reader is seldom left in a state of suspense. There is never any doubt, for instance, at the end of Part IV about the engagement of Lily Dale and Adolphus Crosbie and when Earl De Guest is attacked by a bull, the crisis has passed by the close of the instalment when he has been saved by John Eames. Indeed, in only four parts of the twenty in which the novel was published is there a slight note of tension at the end. But it is in Trollope's next *Cornhill* novel *The Claverings*, a persistently underrated study of Victorian class and sex warfare, that his mastery of the convention of serial writing is most evident. By this stage in his career Trollope had consciously rejected Mrs Gaskell's method of simply ignoring the limitations that the convention placed on a writer and breaking off the story when an instalment had to end, so that serialization had a minimal effect on the novel's form;[43] and similarly, he instinctively avoided Dickens's method of writing in 'blocks' from number to number for sensational effect. He endeavoured instead to utilize the serial divisions in such a way that they contribute to the novel's coherence and unity, while significantly developing its rhetorical design.

Trollope recognized that the serialized novel had to fall into parts coherent enough to stand on their own, for the reader expects the aesthetic satisfaction of contemplating a completed whole. Each number thus presents its own problems of achieving unity and diversity of interest together with a sense of coherent

development. In the first instalment of *The Claverings*, chapters
I–III, where the reader needs an immediate grasp of what the
novel is in the fullest sense 'about', Trollope secures several formal effects to direct our attention to his essential moral concern.
He also gains our interest through the arousal of a strong sense
of expectation and continuity. The number opens on a crisis in
the lives of the novel's central figures as Julia Brabazon coolly
jilts Harry Clavering in the autumnal garden of Clavering Park
in favour of a simply materialistic marriage. Julia's whimsical,
affectionate taunting of Harry with his poverty, his lowly status
as a school usher and his immaturity colours her worldly
cynicism and reveals at the same time the tension of her suppressed love for him; but for her the claims of the inner life
have to yield to those of financial necessity. The burnt grass of
late autumn forms an appropriate background to the end of
their courtship and the more distant emblematic vista of the
square, sombre stone mansion of Sir Hugh Clavering, whose
cynical diplomacy the reader quickly learns is responsible for
the destruction of Harry's youthful hopes, has a significance
which expands as the number progresses. Trollope recognized
the importance of presenting the novel's main concerns as
early and concretely as possible; for while *The Claverings* is a
rich and varied study of Victorian marriage, social class,
materialism and the conflict between youth and age, its organiz-
ing theme, which is placed squarely before the reader in this
opening scene, is the powerful tension between the promptings
of the inner emotions and the diplomatic prudence that rules
Victorian social life. Other interests are interwoven with it,
giving it definition and expanding its significance, but this
important theme is given progressive definition in the remainder
of the number in Julia's careful refusal of Harry Clavering's
rashly proffered life savings to help her out of her financial
plight and in her discussion with her sister, in which she makes
a cold appraisal of the strategic wisdom of her forthcoming
marriage to the infamous Lord Ongar. For as Hermione admits,
her own worldly match with the almost pathological Sir Hugh
Clavering has become a living nightmare.

Trollope's careful balancing of middle class milieux, which

is such an excellent feature of the novel's moral pattern, is also employed to produce an essential measure of unity in the opening instalment. His deft contrast between the rectory, with its well-bred, languid air of untroubled prosperity, the oppressively soulless atmosphere of Clavering Park and the Burtons' lower middle class home at Onslow Crescent, with its busy air of contented domestic routine, serves to articulate his moral vision; for underlying the surface differences of these varied households and marriages there is a powerful similarity of myopic response to the novel's central issue, the tyranny of social will. The constricting ethos of class rigidity which expresses this will is indicated by the dominant subject of the opening instalment, the choice of a career. In the central chapter, 'Harry Clavering chooses his Profession', the rector sneers at his son's choice of a socially demeaning career in civil engineering and, since this occurs after he has been jilted by Julia Brabazon and before her mercenary marriage to the prematurely senile aristocrat, a connection is made by its placing between the flanking chapters which gives a sense of aesthetic completion to the close of the instalment. It does not end on a high note of anticipation, but on a profoundly ironic parallel of character made from Lady Ongar's point of view as she leaves the church after her wedding:

And as she stepped into the chariot which carried her away to the railway station on her way to Dover, she told herself that she had done right. She had chosen her profession, as Harry Clavering had chosen his; and having so far succeeded, she would do her best to make her success perfect. Mercenary! Of course she had been mercenary. Were not all men and women mercenary upon whom devolved the necessity of earning their bread? (p. 32).

Despite the apparent finality of this conclusion, enough narrative hints have been intercalated into the first instalment to ensure the continued interest of the serial reader. There is the measured tone of irony in which Julia Brabazon and Harry Clavering are introduced, there is the early promise of Julia herself, a character too interesting to be lost to the story, and the reader is also informed of her husband's premature senility; then there is the advancement of Harry's career and a hint of development in our knowledge of the unattached status of the Burtons' daughter, Florence. Once the reader has grasped the nature of the potential love triangle he looks forward to further developments in accordance with his well-schooled sense of probability. At the close of the first instalment then, Trollope has achieved the essential serial emotion – a sense of completion together with the tension of foreshadowed development.

However, Trollope was not so much concerned with keeping his reader guessing as with balance and continuity, and he aims at retaining as much of the novel as possible in the reader's consciousness. As he reads on he becomes aware of those various points of interconnection and formal relations of character and situation through which Trollope expresses his moral sense of the underlying sameness of human lives. The major function of this everchanging pattern is to direct the reader to the novel's central concern and to keep it in his view throughout the progress of the serial. All the contrasted marriages of the novel, for instance, are prudent matches based on economic self-interest and at best they are uneasy, diplomatic marriages. The rector's wife has given him up and he feels acutely her lack of respect for him; Cecilia Burton, restive at her husband's humdrum, cautious prudence, engages in a prolonged though unconscious love affair with Harry Clavering (for her efforts to secure him for her sister-in-law go well beyond the bounds of reason and propriety); while Hermione's marriage, which she later bitterly contrasts with that of Mrs Clavering, is a hell of boredom and despair. This pattern of cautious social decorum, personal diplomacy and emotional sterility extends to all the family relations of the novel and Trollope draws attention to these in his chapter titles, which serve as reading directions: 'Sir Hugh and his Brother, Archie', 'Count Pateroff and his Sister'. And indeed, this latter pair, with their comic pseudo-allegorical names, Sophie Gordeloup (gardyloo!) and Count Pateroff (with its hint of cynical sexual conquest) serve, by their almost professional diplomatic expertise, to draw attention to the covert cynicism and inhuman calculation which tarnish English family and social life.

Thus in the early numbers of *The Claverings* Trollope employs a design which creates a formal mnemonic for both author and reader. Once the relation of character or situation has been grasped the appearance of its parallel at a later stage in the serial completes the pattern and bestows on its movement a mnemonic as well as a moral value. The initial impact of this design is made by juxtaposition within the three chapter serial unit. The reader's curiosity is naturally focused on the flanking chapters, each of which is constructed around a coherently developed scene, and the connection between them is made by a reflexive movement of the mind prompted by a sense of closure and completion. In Part II, Chapters IV and VI, 'Florence Burton' and 'The Reverend Samuel Saul', are brought into careful ironic balance because the courtship of Fanny by the curate, who like Harry Clavering wishes to marry his master's daughter, later provides a mirror of the struggle between Harry and Florence Burton. The correspondence is one of character and class reaction. Mr Saul's social concern makes a pointed contrast with Harry Clavering's egoism, while the rector's horror at his curate's effrontery in threatening traditional class boundaries is the response of a narrow class sympathy similar to that shown by Mr Burton. This pattern, lodged early in the reader's mind, is the source of several later ironies when the curate quietly exposes Harry Clavering's bourgeois confusion of social role and moral value as he makes uncomfortably explicit the parallel between them, and when Fanny Clavering's revolt against the outmoded class structure, like her brother's vacillation between Florence and Julia, testifies to a profound emotional hunger which society seeks to deny. Similarly, the instinctive generosity of Florence Burton in her dealings with Harry Clavering and the selfless tact of Mr Saul in his treatment of Fanny, are emphasized when the pattern made in Part II shifts again and Trollope brings them together in mutual recognition of each other's true worth.

However, this is not Trollope's sole technique for securing a formal mnemonic in the serial. He employs the larger elements of form, but often he uses local detail. The habitual action which expresses character can also take on a mnemonic function. Theodore Burton's habit of dusting his boots with his handkerchief is at once an expression of the man and of his class. Harry Clavering in his youthful pride and ignorance substitutes the class image for the man, and refuses to dine with him, and when he does eventually visit the Burtons at Onslow Crescent he cannot imagine how the lovely Cecilia can love a man who dusts his boots in that manner. His response to the Burton household, which moves from condescension to agreeable surprise, is ironically matched by Burton's cool, measured assessment of the interloper, which Trollope sardonically underscores: 'What would Harry have said if he had heard all this from the man who dusted his boots with his handkerchief?' (p. 85). Burton's characteristic habit is referred to repeatedly in Part III so that when the next confrontation between him and Harry Clavering, due to the growing alarm at Onslow Crescent at Harry's estrangement from them, occurs much later in Part IX of the serial (Chapters XXV–XXVII), Trollope can be confident of the mnemonic value of this trait as registering Burton's moral superiority and he calls the chapter simply 'The Man who Dusted his Boots with his Handkerchief'. Here Burton is his wife's diplomatic envoy sent to secure Harry for Florence, and his handling of the meeting with such tact and delicacy creates in Harry Clavering an ironic reversal of his earlier narrow judgement – of which he is embarrassingly conscious: 'And this was the man who had dusted his boots with his pocket-handkerchief, and whom Harry had regarded as being on that account hardly fit to be his friend!' (p. 276).

Trollope secures the variety necessary within the serial instalment to avoid excessive formalism through the mobility of Harry Clavering at the centre of the novel, which is consequent on his crossing class boundaries both in his chosen sphere of work and in his courtship of Florence. In Part III, Chapters VII–IX, Trollope juxtaposes the two moral areas of the novel which make increasingly conflicting claims upon him: the world of Bolton Street where Lady Ongar lives and that of Onslow Crescent, and the third chapter, 'Too Prudent by Half' which closes the number, gains in irony from the preceding closely-linked scenes. Harry's first encounters with the beautiful widowed Lady Ongar and the homely Burtons are thematically important. Harry is dumbfounded by Julia's cynical maturity, her coy appeals to nostalgia and her seductive assault on bourgeois prudery: ' "It is only the world, – Mrs. Grundy, you know, – that would deny me such friendship as yours; not my own taste or choice. Mrs Grundy always denies us exactly those things which we ourselves like best. You are clever enough to understand that" ' (p. 74). From this challenge to the prudent life, diplomatically made, but with an undercurrent of powerful feeling, Harry Clavering has to readjust to meet the world of Onslow Crescent. And Trollope's abrupt change of moral and social atmosphere is masterly. His criticism of puritan materialism is directed precisely at the way it unconsciously informs the lives of warmly realized folk like the Burtons, but to his surprise Harry Clavering finds it attractive. His astonishment at Lady Ongar's altered bearing is matched by the evaporation of his class prejudice as he watches the builder of drains and bridges expertly preparing gravy and decanting wine. But, ironically, although Cecilia ostensibly preaches her husband's conformist work ethic, like Julia Ongar she covertly challenges constricting class claims and also sexual ethics, selecting Harry Clavering as the object of an unconsciously rebellious flirtation. These contending influences, so obviously distinct yet linked by the fundamental need to challenge the crushing power of social will, cancel each other in Harry Clavering's consciousness and the third and closing chapter, 'Too Prudent by Half' is charged with irony as Florence Burton's complacency, nurtured by the materialism and feminine dominance of the bourgeois ethos, prompts her to delay their marriage at the very time when the Burtons' cosy domestic world is being threatened afresh by Lady Ongar, who employs Harry's innate knight-errantry in a romantically diplomatic mission to Count Pateroff.

Harry Clavering's physical movement in the novel is a correlative of his vacillation throughout the serial between the contrary and exclusive choices of a passionless but prudent marriage and a spontaneous but tarnished romance, summarized by these two worlds, geographically placed and related but morally discrete and separate. Such places are part of the formal

mnemonic of the serial because they are the source of the attitudes which the characters carry around with them and which
make such powerful claims on them. But more significantly,
by employing a central and typical figure to link the novel's
different worlds, Trollope solves the serialist's problem of
achieving unity and coherence. Harry Clavering dominates the
first ten of the sixteen instalments and his dilemma focuses
sharply two contemporary human concerns. He is trapped in a
network of rigidly defensive class attitudes which run counter
to economic individualism and the absorption of the middle
classes by the metropolitan mercantile world. And he is also
caught in the clash between society's inflexible idealization of
romantic love and the reality of unpredictable human passions.
He finds it increasingly impossible to distinguish between the
promptings of conscience and of self-interest, between moral
and class values, between love and passion. It is profoundly
ironic that Harry Clavering's dilemma should be the only force
linking the fragmented society of the novel and his faltering
endeavour to vindicate love and social mobility as healing forces
only reveals the more compellingly the slender threads that
connect a community based only on a consensus of will.

Of course Trollope recognized that this method alone is not
enough to guarantee sustained serial interest and the movement
away from Harry Clavering's enveloping point of view is to a
series of alternating actions which are the source of the dominant serial emotion, irony. The management of the transition is
aided by publication in parts, but it is important that such
shifts are smooth if the narrative continuity is not to be lost.
In Part IV, Chapters X–XII, there is the familiar moral pattern
of correspondence between the chapters 'Florence Burton at
the Rectory' and 'Lady Ongar takes possession' and in part this
derives from the basic serial device of the author's and the
reader's omniscience and the characters' ignorance. Florence is
warmly embraced by the fastidious rectory family where she
begins to reap the social benefits of her love, while at Ongar
Park her solitary rival, ostracized by her family and by society
at large, begins to taste the bitter fruit of her more forthright,
calculating materialism. Florence Burton looks to the future

with confidence while Julia Ongar reaches the nadir of despair and self-loathing. The transition in Part IV from Clavering to Ongar Park and away from the centrality of Harry Clavering in the narrative, is made by the central chapter, 'Sir Hugh and his Brother, Archie'. The movement is achieved by means of a split scene which creates a highly formal effect. The fierce quarrel between Sir Hugh Clavering and his uncle, the rector, in the Clavering drawing-room allows Hermione Clavering the opportunity to try to negotiate Harry's agreement to Sir Hugh's mercenary scheme of marrying Julia Ongar to his brother. While the uneasy diplomacy of family life has overtly collapsed and has turned into open wrangling, it is at the same time covertly strengthened by Trollope's emblematic use of the inner room where the dehumanizing bartering with human lives points to the lack of any real moral connection. As Harry Clavering moves from the alcove into the drawing-room there is an ironic correlation of mood between his inner disquiet and their open discord and the irony is underlined by Florence's welcoming smile. But the reader's interest has been firmly located on Julia Ongar and the context of shoddy diplomacy is appropriate to the accompanying movement from the bitter group scene, of which she is the still and invisible centre, to its alienated member; for it is pharisaical social prudence that incarcerates her at Ongar Park and it is to the powerful Sir Hugh Clavering that she owes her position as social victim. Trollope's switching of the reader's vision in the last chapter of the number to Julia Ongar's spiritual desolation means that his gaze can be allowed naturally to rest there as her solitude is next broken by the shadowy figure from her imprisoning past, Count Pateroff.

After Part X the central movement of the serial is furthered by Trollope's method of cross-cutting, which is more than the mechanical alternation of sombre and comic – although this is important for retaining the reader's interest – because it creates a significant ironic pattern. His cross-cutting, for instance, from the conclusion of Part XII when Archie Clavering makes his final comic proposal to Julia Ongar to the tense battle between her and Cecilia Burton at the beginning of Part XIII, is made through the emblematic relations of character and milieu. Archie's club, the Rag, stands for the world of the gaming table and the race-course and he and Cecilia obviously represent different moral areas of Victorian society. Although Archie is shallow and malleable, Trollope does not treat him harshly for he has weighed himself and recognizes his limited moral worth. But Cecilia Burton by contrast possesses the rooted egoism of the novel's varied women, together with the smugness of a moral as-surance bestowed on her by her social background. But although the moral movement from the world of the Rag to that of Onslow Crescent is full and complete, they are deftly linked and com-pared in the ironic juxtaposition of the visits of Archie and Cecilia to Lady Ongar. Archie Clavering's bid for Julia's wealth is at least made open-eyed and with an easy-going cynicism, but Cecilia Burton's wild imprudence is marked by the passion of bitter rivalry. What is more, as Julia Ongar emphasizes to her, the love code she purports to defend in striving to gain Harry Claver-ing for her sister-in-law falsifies human relations. Although both gambles fail, each gambler is given the opportunity to make a fresh moral evaluation. For Archie Clavering it merely brings confirmation of what he already knows, but for Cecilia Burton, blinded by an unacknowledged love for Harry Clavering and by narrow class attitudes, her confrontation with the funda-mental claims of the inner life of the emotions affords her neither moral awakening nor a truthful reassessment of the dangerous realities of feminine power. Trollope stresses the central importance of this power in the world of the novel by his employment of a similar technique in the final instalment. Here, Mrs Clavering's manipulation of her despised husband in order to smooth the way for her children's marriages is ironic-ally juxtaposed with the preceding Chapter XLVI, 'Madame Gordeloup retires from Diplomacy', as Trollope neatly places the subject next to the means of satiric comment. Both women have done untold damage to human relations in the novel, Mrs Clavering from a sense of duty to the binding obligations of the feminine love code and Sophie Gordeloup from a forthright materialism and a frank delight in malice.

The prolonged and frequently interrupted reading of a serial-ized novel means that there is a constant danger that the reader might overlook some important element of the novel's moral pattern, like the quiet contrast which Trollope makes in the opening number between the sisters, Hermione Clavering and Julia Ongar. By the middle of the serial this parallel might have begun to escape the reader's attention and the function of the internal structure of Part VII is to enforce the moral design of their contrasted fortunes, as the death of Hermione's infant son heralds the collapse of her loveless marriage, while Julia Ongar is escaping the claims of her own past and regaining Harry Clavering's love, with its accompanying promise of social acceptance. Then the wheel of fortune, turned as so often in Trollope by social forces, revolves once more under the impetus of feminine diplomatic pressure and at the conclusion of the novel the contrast is made again. This time the context is one of parallel as both sisters, similarly betrayed by society's perverted values, resign themselves to widowhood : the one acutely aware that she has thrown away life's rich possibilities, but morally though not socially redeemed, the other socially irreproachable but still the prisoner of her peevish egoism.

Harry Clavering's sudden capitulation to this powerful collective feminine will, expressed by Florence and Cecilia Burton and by his mother, and subscribed to by the Burton and Clavering families and by the whole ethos of Grundyism which euphemistically cloaks their political will, creates the difficulty of too complete a climax, for his decision to marry Florence comes just over midway through the novel. Trollope handles it with shrewd realism; the unbalancing effect of little Hughy's death, Harry's illness and his mother's bedside intervention on behalf of Florence have psychological weight and truth, but it raises the problem of how to redirect the serial reader's interest and expectations. But because Trollope did not, like Dickens and Thackeray, write from instalment to instalment, he always has such problems under control and he avoids the difficulty by shifting the focus of interest away from Harry Clavering's moral collapse to the society responsible for it. Trollope places his capitulation at the beginning of Part XII and the remainder of the number directs the reader's attention outwards to the wider social movement of the novel; to the parting of Sir Hugh

Clavering and his wife, to Archie Clavering's final visit to Lady Ongar and the growing storm over Fanny's courtship by the curate, so that several issues are kept in suspension for the next instalment.

In *The Claverings* Trollope's serial unit also has several minor but important functions. It is frequently employed to introduce a figure who is later thrown into a dynamic relation with another character, like Florence Burton, whom the practised serial reader could see on Harry Clavering's horizon in Part I; or in Part V, Chapters XIII–XV, when Count Pateroff's mock-sinister diplomacy at the Blue Posts throws in Harry's way the insuperable barriers of the vacuous Doodles and the ponderous military gourmet Colonel Schmoff. The conclusion of a number often assists the reader by establishing the stage reached in Harry Clavering's moral struggle, but it also frequently presents the morally emphatic recognition by a character of some fact or relation previously hidden from him by social manoeuvring or by the engrossing nature of his own egoism. Part II, for instance, ends with Fanny Clavering's startled realization that she is being pursued by her father's curate, a relation which requires the growth of moral sensitivity and self-knowledge. This kind of unwilling recognition is also Julia Ongar's experience at the conclusion of Part IV as loneliness compels her to concede the futility of her materialist ethic. The serial unit also makes a submerged movement in the narrative which creates a subdued but noticeable impact. In the early parts of the serial the central chapter has its own function of introducing new characters, but towards the conclusion it deals with partings and supports the thematic undercurrent of social dislocation. This is elaborated in a series of chapters entitled 'How Damon parted from Pythias', 'Desolation', in which the death of little Hughy creates a vacuum at the heart of the novel, 'Parting', 'How to dispose of a Wife', and 'Showing what happened off Heligoland', in which the death of Sir Hugh Clavering and his brother is reported. And the only central chapter to deal with a reunion, that of Harry and Florence, is given the ironical title, 'The Sheep returns to the Fold'.

One of Trollope's methods for achieving that clear sense of

progression essential for retaining the serial reader's interest is foreshadowing, which creates an ironic perspective within which present actions are given added significance. A major source of anticipation is the repeated situation, which also embodies Trollope's realistic and moral sense of life giving people second chances. As Mr Saul's fortunes are charted against Harry Clavering's throughout the novel, each meeting with Fanny offers the curate a further opportunity to renounce his daring assertion of human values, just as Julia Ongar's return forces Harry Clavering to choose anew between personal and social claims; and while Fanny is repeatedly tempted to betray her class values, Florence Burton is ready to abandon hers. But Trollope's more subtle technique for securing a sense of continuity is his unobtrusive employment of ordinary images which take on the expressive identity of character so that their recurrence later in the serial has a mnemonic effect. They summarize neatly the moral direction of the protagonists at various stages of the story and are carefully intercalated into its varied moral and social contexts. The 'bargain-price-reward' motif, which Julia Ongar eventually learns to transcend, finds its satirical value in the gambling men's talk of the mastery of mares and fillies. But whereas Julia Ongar regarded her marriage as an unpleasant contract, albeit one made on the basis of scarcely concealed cynicism, Captain Boodle and Archie Clavering see marriage in brutal terms as an exciting risk. However, the way in which the novel's women collectively defend the social security afforded by marriage is similarly dehumanizing and is effectively defined by their repeated use of the images of 'sheep' and 'sheep-fold' by which they designate the roles of men and home. This is more insidious because the cosiness of the image falsifies the central importance of the moral and social issues raised by Harry Clavering's dilemma and it masks the energy with which the women govern through the trivialization of urgent human problems. Balancing the 'sheep' imagery is the image of the 'butterfly-in-the-sunshine' used so often by Harry Clavering to describe the superficial attractiveness of his apparent freedom, which is later converted into the truer and more compelling image of the 'moth-and-the-candle'. And there is also the important image foreshadowing an ironical reversal, which Harry Clavering employs when he finally commits himself to Julia Ongar : ' "I must bear what men say. I do not suppose that I shall be all happy, – not even with your love. When things have once gone wrong they cannot be mended without showing the patches. But yet men stay the hand of ruin for a while, tinkering here and putting in a nail there, stitching and cobbling; and so things are kept together. It must be so for you and me" ' (p. 266). This extended image is immediately relevant to all the relationships in the novel, but its potency lies in its reversal in the larger development of the narrative; for while Harry is speaking feminine society is mustering its forces, and it is the women rather than he who patch his relationship, not with Julia Ongar but with Florence Burton, into a superficial whole.

Trollope recognized that towards the conclusion of the serial recollection, aided by the habit of re-reading, is an important source of the reader's moral understanding and in the final instalment of *The Claverings* it creates a profoundly ironic perspective. The encounter of the rivals, Julia Ongar and Florence Burton, is the point to which the reader's anticipation has been directed throughout fifteen instalments and Trollope invests its formal prominence with moral weight. Both Julia and Florence have achieved a measure of moral growth in the course of the novel, Julia through her remorse and her self-sacrifice and Florence through her selfless insight into Harry Clavering's true nature. It is fitting that the only two people who are capable of transcending the limitations of wealth and class and who have been kept apart for so long should finally meet at the conclusion of the novel to revalue their experiences. As in the opening number, Clavering Park forms the consciously ironic background to Julia Ongar's confession of her love :

'It was here, on this spot, that I gave him back his troth to me, and told him that I would have none of his love, because he was poor . . . Now he is poor no longer. Now, had I been true to him, a marriage with him would have been, in a prudential point of view, all that any woman could desire. I gave up the dearest heart, the sweetest temper, aye and the truest man that, that — Well, you have won him instead, and he has been the gainer.' (p. 503).

This explicit acknowledgement of her reversal of fortune binds the serial and invests its conclusion with a moral and aesthetic completeness. But not quite. Behind the bitter, self-mocking irony, containing as it does in her references to Harry Clavering's fidelity and oblique comment on Florence's prudence in marrying him a realistic element of feminine revenge, is concealed nevertheless a sordid world of diplomacy, and Julia Ongar tactfully keeps from the ingenuous girl the shocking truth about the powerful social pressures that, with appalling caprice, have bestowed on her the man she loves. The marriage with which the novel ends is thus not merely a conventional happy ending, nor the pledge to the future or to social harmony that we find in romantic comedy; rather, as the logical conclusion to this subtle study of Victorian class and sex warfare, it is plainly, ironically, and even tragically, inconclusive.

V

THE ACHIEVEMENT

IN THIS concluding chapter I would like to focus attention on the two novels which, in my view, together with such excellent works as *The Last Chronicle of Barset* and *Orley Farm*, will in the long run sustain Trollope's growing reputation among readers and critics alike: *The Way We Live Now* and *The Prime Minister*. Although they develop further several of Trollope's familiar themes which I have already traced in the course of this book – the relation between personal identity and the shaping forces of the environment; the individual's response to the changing values of his society; the tyranny of social convention; problems of will and ambition; the dilemma of the outsider and the highly political nature of English social life – these two novels stand apart not only because they are more artistically conceived, but also because they are rather more profound. After his great success in the 1860s, Trollope had reached a stage in his career when he felt the need to attempt a larger assessment of his age and to make a mature statement about the direction in which he considered English life was moving.

Although *The Way We Live Now* is a masterly satire and *The Prime Minister* is a magnificently documented study of political realism, it would be a mistake to regard their worlds as being totally dissimilar. In the first place *The Way We Live Now* is a good deal less gloomy and *The Prime Minister* is rather more sombre in tone than critics have recognized. And secondly, as I will discuss later, there are grounds for thinking that Trollope regarded them as contiguous and complementary studies of the major sources of power in the modern age, presenting from different perspectives a coherent judgement of Victorian society. Although the majority of Victorians felt that free enterprise and parliamentary government were the twin bulwarks of the English way of life, in these consecutive novels Trollope's detailed examination of their pervasive effects on the whole range of public and private behaviour amounts to a quietly subversive revelation of the moral vacuity and inertia which for him these social systems had come to symbolize.

The Way We Live Now

When it was first published, *The Way We Live Now* was very unpopular. The *Saturday Review*, whose response was fairly typical, objected to 'the incivility of Mr Trollope's title. "The way *we* live!" '[1] But a further reason for its unpopularity may well have been its topicality and uncomfortable relevance. The novel was written at the height of the financial boom of the 1870s and Melmotte's fraudulent venture, the South Central Pacific and Mexican railway, which dominates much of the novel, may have been drawn from the real-life scandal about the misleading prospects of the Honduras Ship Railway, which had failed the previous year. A third reason was undoubtedly the novel's trenchantly satirical tone. Irony governs its texture and is manifested in almost every conceivable form. Most obviously it is present in the title, for far from presenting a celebration of high Victorian progress, the book is overwhelmingly negative. Proposed elopements and marriages fail, the projected railway is, of course, never built, fortunes are not made, since even fraud is ultimately unsuccessful; and after the death of its chief perpetrator, Melmotte, no moral lessons are drawn and social life is allowed to continue as before, ruled by the same sordid conventions. Essentially the novel is characterized by the way people conspicuously fail to achieve anything even in their own strictly limited terms.

However, perhaps a more fundamental reason for the lack of success of *The Way We Live Now* with contemporary readers is the way that Trollope's irony continually disrupts the relation between the author and the reader. There is a disturbing ambivalence between the expectations which a practised Trollope reader brings to the novel and the authorial stance implied in the title. On the one hand there is an element of reassurance for the reader in Trollope's satiric exaggeration, as for instance in his handling of Melmotte's preposterous dinner for the Emperor of China, but on the other hand his sense of moral security is upset by the author's balancing technique of understatement, for example in his treatment of the spiritual poverty of the Church. And there resides an equally disturbing use of irony in Trollope's treatment of character. His reader's anticipation of the familiar many-sided study of individual moral dilemmas as people strive to achieve an equable relation with their society is frustrated because in *The Way We Live Now* people's problems are simply 'operational' – purely political dilemmas of how to gain some personal advantage or neutralize attacks on their social positions. The reader is thus left striving to read moral situations of which Trollope's characters stubbornly refuse to admit the existence. And this absence of firm authorial guidance creates a disorienting experience akin to that of the figures within the world of the novel itself. In several respects, therefore, and not least in the way Trollope has cut his reader adrift, *The Way We Live Now* is a self-consciously modern novel.

Trollope himself, overreacting as he sometimes did to criticism, remarked that the novel contained good satire but was too exaggerated.[2] However, it is by no means wholly satiric. Indeed, as we have already observed, as a realist and a moralist Trollope strenuously eschewed simple moral absolutes and while his satiric assault on modern capitalism and its ethos is powerfully substantiated in its own terms, the world which he thus exposes for our judgement is inhabited by ordinary, frail men and women trying to do their best for themselves and their families in a time of great social flux and moral uncertainty. There are, moreover, gleams of sanity and goodness as the world that Trollope presents is endlessly qualified and humanized. Melmotte is clearly a modern monster, but he is equally a naïve and pathetic victim;

Mr Longestaffe's harsh, confused morality is shown to proceed from his sense of being stranded between the old world and the new; while the unscrupulous Lady Carbury achieves a muted kind of redemption through her love for her unworthy son. The satiric force of *The Way We Live Now* is thus balanced by Trollope's simultaneous provision of a wonderfully realistic and delicate treatment of human problems which evokes a large measure of sympathy for little people trapped by historical circumstances beyond their understanding or control. Trollope does not, however, shirk the implications of his satire and allow the novel to veer towards comedy and comic solutions as James R. Kincaid suggests; rather, in my view, he manages to combine, without any sense of strain, both an absolutist moral stance and a high degree of moral relativism.[3] He recognizes that people both make and are made by their society and that the individual's crucially important struggle to assert and maintain his identity through marriage, business, or politics now takes place within a dangerously uncertain environment and is subject to altered pressures. Of course, to the extent that people and institutions are responsible for creating a malevolent social ethos they are vulnerable to the scourge of the satirist, but equally, when they are forced by society to consistently deny their individuality so that life becomes devoid of meaning for them, our response must be one of sympathy.

The main focus of Trollope's satire is the capitalist system, which in his view had fostered an increasingly intense struggle for wealth and power; however, his venom includes not only the entrepreneurial class, represented by Melmotte,[4] but the parasitic establishment figures like the Grendalls and also the multiple moral failure of social institutions such as the Church, the political parties, the city and the press, all of which either openly or covertly support the debased values which Melmotte stands for. Even more painful for contemporary readers must have been the way that Trollope's remorselessly logical analysis of the way in which the money ethic has permeated human affairs destroys a whole collection of cherished myths – the puritan work ethic; the doctrine of self-help and social mobility; the belief in the heroic qualities of the captains of industry and commerce; the aristocratic creed of *noblesse oblige*; the comforting faith in the sanctity of true love and domestic bliss; or the lingering notion that England was still a Christian country – all of which have been swept away.

Because, in the modern world life is no longer fruitful or joyous, but fraught with anxiety and despair, the novel is full of unnatural relations. Women like Madame Melmotte, Lady Pomona, Lady Carbury and Mrs Hurtle are or have been terrified or humiliated by their bullying husbands; children like Lord Nidderdale and Marie Melmotte are pawns in their parents' struggle to accumulate wealth and position; alternatively, like Felix Carbury, they cold-bloodedly batten on their parents, or, if like Dolly Longestaffe they have financial independence, they are rebellious and unloving; while lovers such as Marie Melmotte, Hetta Carbury, Mrs Hurtle and John Crumb are deceived and jilted. Two examples in particular demonstrate the perversion of human relations that occurs when social pressures override the need for self-determination. For the Victorians it would not have been uncommon to find a member of the impoverished squirearchy like Mr Longestaffe trying to make a financially sound match for his daughter, but the reader is astonished and disturbed to discover that she feels constrained to engage actively in selling herself. Still more interesting is the relation between Lord Nidderdale and Melmotte towards the close of the novel. The lonely city magnate is so far gone in lies and illusions that he can gain satisfaction even from a 'simulated confidence' with the young man (II, 225). But this perverted psychology, which suddenly and surprisingly humanizes Melmotte, testifies to the underlying need of people even as thoroughly cynical as the great financier himself, to make an intimate human contact for, as Trollope is concerned to demonstrate throughout the novel, people cannot for ever escape the claims of their own humanity.

Yet for the most part people have become so conditioned to the impersonal ethic of free enterprise that they are only dimly aware of the extent to which, within little more than a generation, it has transformed English life. The modern world is urban, secular and capitalist and the old moral values of the Christian order of Barsetshire, although still alive vestigially in people's language and frame of reference, have been overlaid by a new and frightening nihilism. As Hetta Carbury recognizes, there has come into being 'a newer and worse sort of world' to which they all now belong (I, 71). Throughout the novel Trollope juxtaposes the old values and the new in a surprisingly extensive satirical counterpoint of patterns of animal and biblical imagery in order to chart this shift in the whole spiritual frame of the contemporary world. The competitive commercial ethic has produced a post-Darwinian social jungle. Indeed, the young men of the Beargarden Club frankly admit that they inhabit a world in which people 'prey on each other'. The arch-capitalist Melmotte is described variously as a 'commercial cormorant', or a 'wolf and a vulture', who would skin people if he could get money for their carcases. And his aristocratic 'curs', Lord Alfred Grendall and his son, denounce him as a 'brute'. The wild American, Winifred Hurtle who, like Melmotte, is in love with power, is defined by a similar cluster of images as a 'wild-cat', a 'tigress' and a 'beast of prey'. It follows that in this world those who are not predators are victims. Lady Carbury offers herself to her son like a 'pelican' and in return is tortured by him like a 'butterfly upon a wheel'. A corollary of this general process of dehumanization is that people now display the whole range of animal instincts. Felix Carbury, for instance, who is judged by his uncle to possess the 'instincts of a horse', turns a social event into an act of bestiality, asking his mother when the 'animals' are coming to 'feed'. And Madame Melmotte observes, after deriding Marie as a 'pig, ass, toad, dog' when she refuses to be sold into marriage, that even love is simply a 'beastly business'.

Indeed, there is a profound absence of any significant inner life in most of these new people and Trollope's contrapuntal pattern of biblical imagery indicates the moral and spiritual frame that they have abandoned. Lady Carbury, who like the Longestaffes occasionally attends church when in the country where it is still a mark of class and fashion, is merely doing her social duty by discussing her soul with the surprised Bishop of Elmham. We also learn that Felix Carbury and Georgiana

Longestaffe never read the Bible and that the American entrepreneur Mr Fisker has never prayed in his life. Moreover, when
the Bible is referred to, it is invoked in the strict service of self-
interest. Lady Carbury employs it in defence of her son's idleness
(I, 364), while Lady Pomona uses it to buttress her opposition to
her daughter's marriage with a Jew (II, 263). In reply Georgiana
turns the Scriptures against her parents, accusing them of feed-
ing her stones and serpents (II, 424). Surprisingly, one of the few
people who does read the Bible and who even quotes it to the
astonished Felix Carbury, is the amiable young Lord Nidderdale,
but his belief in refraining from throwing the first stone is really
little more than a variation of Beargarden hedonism (I, 209).

In Trollope's view the modern world has abandoned the
Christian faith for a new religion. It now 'worships' Melmotte
(I, 331) whose faith is utilitarian and materialistic: 'It seemed
that there was but one virtue in the world, commercial enterprise, – and that Melmotte was its prophet' (I, 411). Because
people vaguely sense that they are stranded between two worlds
they look to men like Melmotte to give a spiritual dimension
to the new commercial order so as to allay their profounder
apprehension of the appalling emptiness of their lives, and their
thwarted religious instinct thus finds a new and perverted mode
of expression. But the main symbolic role that Trollope assigns
to Melmotte, ironically, is that of the Tempter, whose success
represents nothing less than man's second Fall. This satirical
function grows unobtrusively out of local, realistic detail. Melmotte's inversion of the whole moral order is quietly suggested
by his habit of conducting business on Sundays and by the way
in which, both as a social entertainer and as a forger, he turns
night into day. As Melmotte's reputation grows, Mr Longestaffe
comes to feel that he is a great 'necromancer' and a Medea
figure, and the theme of conjuring is sustained by the grand
illusion of 'fairyland' that Melmotte creates for the great ball
(I, 115). Hints of the diabolical also accumulate throughout the
novel until they constitute one of its central satirical statements,
as the black magician is gradually transformed into the devil
himself. Melmotte's wife, for instance, believes that he is as
'powerful as Satan', while the lawyer Mr Squercum regards

himself as the 'destroying angel of this offensive dragon' (II, 258, 230). Indeed, in several important respects Melmotte's career makes a parallel with that of Milton's Satan. Driven by the law from a life of luxury on the Continent where he had finally overreached himself, Melmotte seeks to build his own kingdom in London, Trollope's modern hell. He re-establishes authority over the social world through his cohorts Lord Alfred Grendall and his son by the sheer force of his egoism, and the illusion of unlimited power that he creates is given a defiantly symbolic presence when he has his own Pandemonium built for the great dinner. Yet although Melmotte regards himself as the absolute ruler of his kingdom, the city, and as a god-like being who can dine with the brother of the Sun, once more like Satan he falls through overweening pride as he comes 'almost to believe in himself' (II, 20, 57). And this symbolic pattern is extended to include the Beargarden Club, several of whose members have been drawn into Melmotte's financial orbit; for at the closing of the club, which coincides with Melmotte's death, Mr Lupton ironically describes it as a Paradise that they have forfeited, while the religiously inclined Lord Nidderdale meditates with unconsciously dark humour on the consequences of the fall of Adam (II, 431, 437).

Although Trollope's satiric use of biblical parallels emphasizes the perversion of values in contemporary life most people cannot give proper expression to the change that they feel has taken place. Mrs Hurtle, an American and an outsider, is the exception. She frankly celebrates the alteration. Indeed, she is Melmotte's chief apologist, defending him and the system he represents in almost Nietzschean terms and affording it a quasi-spiritual dimension. What she worships in him is the will to power, comparing his stature with that of George Washington and Napoleon. Such a man, she says, rises above mere honesty because power transcends morality. And it is Mrs Hurtle who makes explicit Trollope's interest in the connection between the exercise of power in the modern world and the mythology of heroic capitalism, because she believes that 'wealth is power, and that power is good' (I, 246). Moreover, in her view, commercial power greatly outweighs that of mere politicians or political systems.

One of the fundamental ironies of the novel is the way that not only English society but Melmotte himself become the willing victims of this superficially attractive philosophy. The American entrepreneur Hamilton K. Fisker puffs him up into a commercial 'hero' and when he entertains the Emperor of China he is finally accepted as such by the nation (II, 45). And because he aims at unlimited power, he inevitably also endeavours to become a 'political hero' (II, 171). But Melmotte eventually finds himself trapped by the myth-making process. When his fraud is discovered and his career is finished, he still feels hopeful that he may yet be able to transform himself into a criminal hero so that his reputation 'would not all die' (II, 298). And he eventually chooses suicide partly so that something of the mythology he has striven to create may remain intact.

However, before he dies Trollope allows us a rare interior view of this enigma, partly in order to satirize the popular Victorian myth of social mobility based on economic individualism by revealing that instead of being a Dick Whittington figure, Melmotte is an obscure, illegitimate, foreign Jew, who has scaled the pinnacle of the English commercial world by manipulating its rapacity and credulity. But the central thrust of Trollope's satire is directed at the fact that, like the traditional hero figure, Melmotte symbolizes his society's values. In truth people have created him out of their own deepest needs, both material and spiritual, and just as his reputation for wealth and power depends upon his exploitation of society he is in turn a creature of its collective will, its servant and victim as well as its leader and hero.

If Melmotte provides the measure by which Trollope intends us to judge English life, we must take into account the important American element in the novel, which critics have tended to overlook, in order to assess the significance of what Melmotte represents, for to witness free enterprise in its most modern form we must look not to Melmotte but to Fisker. And in this connection Trollope's formal mastery coincides with his satiric intentions, because while Melmotte stands at the heart of the novel linking all its characters in his web of commerce, Fisker remains in the shadows on the novel's periphery. Melmotte represents the older order of European capitalism, bound up with quasi-spiritual needs, with the social mythologies and complex traditions that finally baffle him. Fisker on the other hand, exemplifies how insidious and unheroic the new form of free enterprise really is. Unlike the lugubrious, monosyllabic Melmotte in whom we witness the machinery of commerce ponderously at work, Fisker is mercurial, good-humoured and intelligently audacious. An instinctive manipulator, he first selects the respectable Paul Montague as a dummy director in order to gain credence for the proposed railway venture and then employs the wealthy Melmotte to attract needy men of rank to its board in order to complete the cosmetic operation. After the financial débâcle in London he is still around to pick up the pieces, turning the failure of the company in Europe into the making of its San Francisco branch and walking off with Marie Melmotte's fortune into the bargain. He is the new international man, acutely aware that San Francisco is now a suburb of London and that he can play off England against America in order to facilitate a rise in his railway shares. The American element in the novel is important primarily because it demonstrates how England is being sucked into the much larger world of western capitalism with its brutal realism and frontier ethics. For all his cosmopolitanism and arrogance, Melmotte, like the English, is essentially provincial and naïve. And this is his undoing. He becomes obsessed, not only with the creation of his own mythology, but with the class system of his adopted country, making fatal errors of judgement about the power of rank before the law and misjudging too the inbuilt strength of its snobbery, which effectively excludes him from society's inner circles. Fisker, by contrast, never makes the mistake of believing in the myths that he assiduously cultivates and it is his anonymity and his clinical manipulation of the system and its figureheads on an international scale that make him and his kind so dangerously invulnerable and modern. If Melmotte is Trollope's yardstick for the decline in the English way of life, Fisker represents his grim warning about the direction in which he felt contemporary society was inevitably moving.

The urgency of Trollope's prophetic note is intensified by his examination of the tyranny that the free enterprise system exerts over English life. One of his chief satiric triumphs in *The Way We Live Now* is his revelation of the way in which the ethic of the market-place has so permeated people's consciousnesses that ordinary intercourse has come to obey the impersonal laws of supply and demand. The strongholds of traditional values, the Church, the political parties, the press, marriage and social gatherings have degenerated into areas where human value is measured in cash. Just as in the commercial world the rising price of Melmotte's railway shares is based on his conjectured wealth and their fall is contingent on the collapse of this illusion, so in private society tickets for his grand dinner stand 'very high in the market' until the last moment when rumours of an impending social fiasco cause their value to plummet (II, 88). Even friendship is shown to be subject to the same impersonal laws as Lady Monogram trades her social assistance to Georgiana Longestaffe in return for her allocation of tickets, feeling that she has been cheated in her bargain when they turn out to be worthless. More poignantly, Georgiana, who has always overvalued herself in the marriage market, desperately lowers her price as she grows older. Parallels such as these, which are multiplied in the novel, record how people have traded away their precious individuality, reducing themselves in the process to the status of vulnerable objects.

Money permeates the atmosphere of *The Way We Live Now*. It is the focus of people's aspirations and fears. We learn how much they earn writing novels and newspaper articles, how much they sell their homes for and what they win or lose at gaming or in the share market. Trollope's detailed realism allows the neutrality of cash to stand as an important ironic symbol for personal relations in the modern world and as such it makes most of the formal connections between them, throwing into weird juxtaposition widely diverse areas of society. But at least money is in a sense real. Credit, which in fact effectively governs people's behaviour, is not. Melmotte's wealth is a carefully fostered illusion, sustained by the community and subject to rumour. Trollope exploits for satiric effect the parallel between the spurious activities of Melmotte's railway board and the ceaseless gambling at the Beargarden Club. The one deals in worthless share scrips, the other in valueless IOUs. Just as people fear that Paul Montague will reveal that Melmotte is a swindler, nobody at the Beargarden wishes to know that Miles Grendall cheats at cards, for these acts would involve the acknowledgement of a real world of solid objects and moral absolutes that must be suppressed. Trollope maintains the contrapuntal relation between these two groups throughout the novel, for the existence of the one is dependent on the social currency of the other, and the collapse of Melmotte's empire coincides with the closing of the club. By this neat but entirely natural formal parallel, Trollope emphasizes the fundamental irony that in reality the doctrine of economic individualism rests on a mindless conformism. Indeed, the most chillingly ironic statement in the entire novel comes from Melmotte as he instructs his railway board in the morality of free enterprise: 'Unanimity', he intones, 'is the very soul of these things' (I, 381).

This flight from reality is evident not only in the larger social world but in its microcosmic symbol, the Beargarden Club, where it is focused more intensely. Bereft of moral conviction and lacking faith in themselves and in society alike, the young men evade the truth about the awful hollowness of their existence by regarding life as a tedious game. The game, indeed, emerges as a potent metaphor for the nihilism of the new world. In the competition for the 'Marie Melmotte Plate', Felix Carbury feels himself to have been 'checkmated' by her father, but nevertheless he decides to 'carry on the game' (I, 223; II, 154); Lord Nidderdale wants to enter business simply because commerce might prove more exciting than whist or loo (II, 225); while for Dolly Longestaffe even Melmotte's suicide is less awful than having nothing to amuse him (II, 433). This shocking reduction of death to the level of a game of cards demonstrates how formidable are the barriers erected against the intrusion of moral reality. The notion of the game not only serves to orchestrate the competitive elements of social life, creating a buffer against uncomfortable truths, but it affords at the same time a set of rules that effectively absolves the players from individual responsibility.

Much of the burden of Trollope's satire lies heavily on the governing classes represented by the Longestaffes, the Monograms, the Nidderdales and the Grendalls, whose misplaced pride in their rank and their need to maintain it with acquired cash turn them into Melmotte's bitterly resentful lackeys. And there is a high irony in the fact that Melmotte covets English titles and distinctions which Trollope shows to be debased. But his satire casts a wide net and there is a characteristic double-edged irony in the way he offers Mrs Hurtle as a symbol of emancipated American womanhood for our judgement, while employing her at the same time as a vehicle for his criticism of English life. Her commitment to energy and freedom from conventional constraints comes as a breath of fresh air blowing through the novel. She argues with conviction precisely what Trollope demonstrates, that in England the possibility for the kinds of achievement she advocates is limited by the laws of inheritance which prevent young noblemen from becoming their own masters; by a class system which fosters marriages based on rank and wealth; by the way women are repressed and subdued and by the manner in which English social life is governed by the trivial canons of good taste. As an independent outsider she is an accurate analyst but her conclusion that England is a 'soft civilization' is underwritten by the fact that she is in love with several aspects of English life and by those qualities that she exemplifies in her personal relations (I, 445).

However, as I suggested earlier, Trollope's world is not totally dark, nor is it treated in a uniformly satirical way, for *The Way We Live Now* also contains a realistic examination of human dilemmas intensified by a period of great flux. Because people often find themselves in situations not of their own choosing and from which there is little possibility of escape there is a moral relativism and sympathy at the heart of Trollope's judgement of character which makes allowances for the oppressive influence of the new environment. Mr Longestaffe's offensive treatment of his daughter's suitor, the honourable Jew Mr Brehgert, contrasts strongly with his dealings with the evil Jew Melmotte, to whom he is prepared to sell his birthright, Pickering. Longe-staffe's situation is a subtle study of racial hatred and moral confusion, but it is qualified by the fact that he feels himself to be trapped by circumstances beyond his control. Indeed, by a curious twist of psychology he even takes pride in his depressed condition because it both confirms his status as being above that of the rich parvenus and justifies his inertia and his appalling prejudices. And in his misconceived loyalty to the past, Longe-staffe makes a surprising parallel with Roger Carbury, Trollope's moral norm in the novel, who is nevertheless perverse in his insistence in handing on Carbury Manor to his nephew, who is certain to ruin the property, simply from a blind reverence for tradition. But although both men exhibit a moral smugness that Trollope finds distasteful, he understands their instinctive grasping at the old ways. And not only the gentry, but self-consciously modern people are also muddled by the changing times. Although as an American Mrs Hurtle cherishes her love of heroism and power, at the same time her woman's instinct for self-sacrifice leads her into a love affair with an effete young Englishman who in her heart she despises. But because, like Roger Carbury, she is morally alert she recognizes the powerful irony at work in the contrary impulses that chart her moral confusion. However, for the most part people are intensely aware of the desperate nature of their predicaments without being able to apply to them any moral remedies. The reader watches the way individuals become trapped in situations by a remorseless logic that proceeds out of the way they live. Often such dilemmas arise from their inability to recognize moral claims. Georgiana Longestaffe, for instance, loses Mr Brehgert because of her prolonged, mercenary negotiations over his Lon-don house, a course which is consistent with her market phil-osophy and is a source of dark humour. But like most of the novel's characters, she is not treated as a tragic figure because she regards herself as a marketable commodity and thus denies her selfhood.

All Trollope's varied patterns of character and situation serve to stress how moral alternatives are restricted by the new environment, how individual growth is warped or stunted and how idealism founders. There is the parallel between Ruby Ruggles, the servant girl, and Georgiana Longestaffe who both come up to London from the country husband-hunting among men of rank and fortune and have to be schooled into the realistic limitations of age, class and the treachery of the metropolitan world. But the fundamental irony for people living in an atomistic society is that they have to face their problems alone, unaware that other people confront similar dilemmas. Trollope employs his familiar pattern of rotating stories to record the bleak uniformity of this world and of the pressures that can overwhelm the isolated individual, and this is a profound source of the reader's sympathy. This is particularly true of the main victims in the novel, its various women. Like Lady Carbury, Mrs Hurtle fights to overcome the plight of the single woman in a predatory society and both of these women are finally redeemed. But perhaps a closer and more surprising parallel is that between Winifred Hurtle and Marie Melmotte. The only women in possession of independent fortunes and the freedom to assert their right to self-determination, they chart the lonely struggle of romantic idealism. At the opening of the novel no two people are more dissimilar, the one a fierce, widowed American and the subject of scandal, the other a timid, young European Jewess. But both share the feminine instincts which girls like Georgiana Longestaffe and her English sisters have long ago learnt to suppress. And although their golden idols, as Marie Melmotte calls Felix Carbury, turn to clay, they love the clay nevertheless, only to be bitterly disillusioned. These women of spirit (for Marie Melmotte matures rapidly during the course of the novel) also offer independently judgements of English life which coincide with telling effect. Ironically the European Jewess comes to feel degraded by her contact with the aristocracy, while the American regards society as being in the grip of a terrible paralysis. But they cannot escape, as Hetta Carbury can, to the rural world of Suffolk. For them America, with all its vulgarity and violence, offers the only, tainted alternative and soured and despairing, their final escape there at the close of the novel in the company of Fisker constitutes their muted tragedy.

Such people require our sympathy, and in the course of the novel Mrs Hurtle is transformed from a satirical symbolic force into a woman distinguished by her capacity to care. Similarly, false and foolish though she is, Lady Carbury also has claims on our compassion because of the rare naturalness of her love for her worthless son. And Trollope has considerable residual sympathy too for the young men of the Beargarden who are not entirely wicked or vicious, but whose lives are cramped and empty of purpose. However, the main sympathetic figure, who recognizes moral problems for what they are and acts accordingly, is the traditional Trollopian character, Roger Carbury. His rural world is Trollope's only viable alternative to the modern age and the centrifugal form of the novel, radiating out from Melmotte at its centre, demonstrates how the rural characters on its periphery are sucked into the tainted London world. Father Barham, the priest, is duped by Melmotte's display of wealth, while the servant, Ruby Ruggles, is dazzled by Felix Carbury's rank. But Roger Carbury remains undeceived. He cares deeply about people and although he is portrayed as crusty, romantic and sententious, putting himself in the wrong with Paul Montague and making a fool of himself over Hetta Carbury, he is ruled by good nature and good sense. He represents the old-fashioned Christian virtues exemplified by his traditional Anglicanism, his acts of practical charity and by his position as the figurehead of a close-knit community rooted in the permanence of the Church and the land. Of course Trollope does not offer us rural Suffolk as the perfect pre-lapsarian world. It is a backwater, out of touch with changing times and all it can hold out as an alternative to an atomistic, nihilistic society is an outdated feudalism. Just as Trollope's treatment of American values constitutes his warning about the future, Suffolk is his nostalgic picture of what society has irretrievably forsaken.

Although Trollope has produced a novel in which moral laws appear to be in abeyance, it does not follow that they no longer exist, or have no force. As I have been arguing, *The Way We Live Now* combines a satirical, absolutist stance with the creation of a realistic moral world in which unnaturalness cannot for long be sustained without some form of retribution. This arises logically out of human behaviour and Lady Carbury's book, 'The Wheel of Fortune' provides an appropriate symbol not only for her own life but for the working out of the process of natural justice in the world. This creates a pattern which is best realized in the meteoric rise and fall of the novel's central figure, Melmotte. It grows naturally out of his whole way of life. He is brought down by a paradox of the system by which he lives. When he most desperately needs money to pay off the purchase of Pickering, rumour of his debts and the consequent fall of his railway shares prevent him from raising the necessary capital. And although he has used his daughter as his private bank, she chooses the moment of his greatest need to assert her personal independence. What is more, he becomes the victim of his own strategy of total deceit, because by the time she realizes that for the first time her father is telling the truth her decision to help him comes too late. Moreover, his contemptuous forging of Dolly Longestaffe's signature to the title deeds proceeds from the fact that he is cocooned in a world of illusion which is ironically shattered by Dolly's unshakeable adherence to reality. But the most telling irony of all is the fact that since in Melmotte's world everything, including human life, has a market value, when he becomes aware that his own has fallen to zero he accepts the brutal logic of the market-place and commits suicide. And it is at this point that we realize with a shock that he scarcely existed at all in his own right, but primarily as the expression of an impersonal social will.

All the other major characters suffer similar profound reversals of fortune. There is a dark irony in the fact that the Jewish banker Mr Brehgert judges Georgiana Longestaffe to be too mercenary for him. Unable to believe that he could wish to be free of a high-born Christian lady her failure is terrible to her and faced with the reality of age and loneliness she despairingly runs off with a penniless curate. She pays the penalty for her willing acquiescence in the destruction of human values, not, however, in the sufferings of conscience, for repentance is bound up with the kind of moral awareness that is largely absent from this novel, but from a clear recognition of life's missed opportunities. And this pattern is multiplied. For all her idealism, Mrs Hurtle believes at heart in the supremacy of the will and she is constrained by this to try to intimidate Paul Montague. But because he prefers softer women this very procedure guarantees her failure. However, for Lady Carbury the wheel of fortune is turned by the power of love and this is sufficiently rare in the novel to draw attention to itself. In spite of her mercenary nature, her hypocrisy and her pathetic attempts to manipulate editors, her sacrificial love for her son, which Trollope describes as 'pure and beautiful', is the one redeeming feature of her character which attracts Mr Broune and results in his proposal of marriage (II, 211). This change in fortune is accompanied by a moral growth as she repents her past life, echoing Thackeray's narrator in *Vanity Fair*, as having been 'all vanity, – and vanity, – and vanity !' (II, 462). She recognizes the falsity and emptiness of her life, the poverty of her literary talent and her cruel neglect of her daughter. Her worthless son is taken off her hands and unlike almost all the other characters she is enabled to make an optimistic start to a new life based on sober moral realism.

It was not for nothing that Trollope had originally designated Lady Carbury as his 'chief character'.[5] She dominates the opening of the novel and strikes its satirical keynote. But as it progresses Melmotte becomes the organizing centre of Trollope's satire, while Lady Carbury forms the focal point of the group of character relations which belongs to the novel's realistic mode, which humanizes it and softens the absolutism of its satire. More importantly, in a world in which people's continual mortgaging of the present for an uncertain future, fostered by the competitive system that they have brought into being, merely guarantees frustration, Lady Carbury's experience offers the promise of a kind of redemption and the continuation of basic human goodness. Trollope's hope for the future lies not in the old ways of life that Roger Carbury represents, but in man's recognition that the prolonged abrogation of moral and spiritual values against his own deepest instincts is futile and self-defeating.

The Prime Minister

It is remarkable that a contemporary critic should have regarded Trollope's masterpiece as marking his 'decadence', but in fact the *Saturday Review* again condemned it as severely as it had his previous novel and the other reviews were almost universally unfavourable.[6] This may have been due partly to the fact that, although it maintains a consistently realistic tone and there is a marked absence of satire. Trollope's account of Victorian political life in *The Prime Minister* is more deeply pessimistic than his treatment of the free enterprise society in *The Way We Live Now*. However, his examination of the ways in which capitalism and parliamentary government fail to fulfil human aspirations are not documentary studies but rather parables of the modern age. But although Palliser's Coalition Government has no greater historical authenticity than Melmotte's railway board, both function as large metaphors for the real world and of course, as several critics have observed, in *The Prime Minister* Trollope draws on Victorian politics in the interests of realism, mediating imperceptibly throughout the novel between fiction and history.

Because, in these novels, Trollope is concerned with different aspects of what is essentially the same world, he creates several links between them. Most obvious is his introduction into *The Prime Minister* of a younger Melmotte in the person of Ferdinand Lopez, the Portuguese Jewish speculator. Although more humanized, anglicized and sophisticated than Melmotte, like the great financier, he is, Trollope tells us, 'a self-seeking, intriguing adventurer, who did not know honesty from dishonesty when he saw them together' (I, 275). Both men are absorbed in the struggle to gain admission into English society and both in their different ways try to use marriage as a route to social status and wealth. Moreover, both strive to enter Parliament and when their careers finally crash in ruins both commit suicide. Fundamentally, both men are given the function of testing the values of English life and in *The Prime Minister*, as in *The Way We Live Now*, the outsider is the main linking agent in the novel. Not only is Lopez the centre of the important subsidiary plot, but his attempt to carve a place for himself in society brings him into contact with virtually the whole spectrum of the Victorian world: the middle class strongholds of the Whartons and the Fletchers, the seedy city world of Sexty Parker, the subterranean world of the working classes represented by Tenway Junction, and the politico-social arena of the Prime Minister himself, Gatherum. However, unlike Melmotte, the younger man employs traditional English methods to obtain his goal by marrying into the moneyed middle classes. But because Lopez tries to behave like an English gentleman he is much more vulnerable than Melmotte, and Trollope's scrutiny of the various ways Lopez is snubbed and thwarted, for all the wrong reasons, makes this novel more disillusioning than *The Way We Live Now*.

The contiguity of these two novels is also suggested by Trollope's repeated use of the 'special case', which he employs for satiric effect in the former novel, but with even more devastating realism in *The Prime Minister*. He does so in order to reveal disturbing truths about the fundamental nature of power. In the earlier novel his placing of a brutal figure at the pinnacle of English commercial life constitutes a satiric indictment of the tyrannical system under which people are content to live. By contrast, in *The Prime Minister*, Trollope selects as his representative political figurehead his ideal statesman, Plantagenet Palliser and puts him in charge of the best Government, theoretically, that can be devised, a non-partisan Coalition serving the national interest, which nevertheless fails from a lack of political will. But like Melmotte, Palliser quickly discovers the limits and the ultimate futility of power. Indeed, in both novels real power is shown to be elusive, for both Melmotte and Palliser are really the instruments of others, of Hamilton K. Fisker and the Duke of St Bungay. But in the broader sense, too, they are agents of their society and when they are no longer useful as credible figureheads, its communal assent is withdrawn and they fall.

Although, like Walter Bagehot with whom he has been frequently compared, Trollope regarded politics on one level as an exciting game and Parliament as the best club in London, more importantly he shared with his fictional Prime Minister two unshakeable convictions; first, that 'to serve one's country without pay is the grandest work that a man can do, – that of all studies the study of politics is the one in which a man may make himself most useful to his fellow-creatures'; and second, that his position as an 'advanced conservative Liberal' was the most rational that could be held.[7] Although they are meliorists, both Palliser and Trollope are more in sympathy with the whole movement towards democracy than was Bagehot, for instance.[8] Trollope's statement of his belief in political evolution in his *Autobiography* – that while Conservatives wish to maintain social distances, the Liberal 'is alive to the fact that these distances are day by day becoming less, and he regards this continual diminution as a series of steps towards that human millennium of which he dreams' – is amplified by his Prime Minister in a rare moment of confidence to the astonished Phineas Finn:

Equality would be a heaven, if we could attain it. How can we to whom so much has been given dare to think otherwise? How can you look at the bowed back and bent legs and abject face of that poor ploughman, who winter and summer has to drag his rheumatic limbs to his work, while you go a-hunting or sit in pride of place among the foremost few of your country, and say that it all is as it ought to be? You are a Liberal because you know that it is not all as it ought to be, and because you would still march on to some nearer approach to equality . . . (II, 321–2).[9]

However, one of the novel's central ironies is the fact that Palliser's innate diffidence will not permit him to fire men with speeches like this in the House. His political dream is too private for the hurly-burly of parliamentary debate and it therefore resists translation into dynamic political action.

Several critics, including Bradford Booth, Robert Polhemus, Ruth apRoberts and John Halperin, have debated the success or failure of Palliser's political career.[10] However, for me, and I think for Trollope too, that is not the strictly relevant issue. For all its political realism, *The Prime Minister* is a parable and in it Trollope employs the 'special case' – the unique conjunction of his ideal statesman with a Coalition Government – in order to reveal the processes of Victorian political life as a way of assessing the political health of the nation. He creates a situation in which there exists the possibility of a truly representative, patriotic Government guided by reason and led by an unambitious, conscientious statesman. However, in spite of the old Duke's claims that the Government has achieved the limited success he anticipated, Trollope shows how in meaningful political terms it has failed conclusively and how Palliser's hopes of doing something grand for his country are dashed. The failure is the result of the clash between Palliser's character and the nature of political reality. As Trollope tells us in his *Autobiography*, his ideal statesman lacks moral elasticity : 'I had . . . conceived the character of a statesman [as being] superior . . . But he should be scrupulous, and, as being scrupulous, weak.'[11] And this judgement is endorsed by Trollope's political realist, the Duke of St Bungay, who remarks that Palliser 'has but one fault, – he is a little too conscientious, a little too scrupulous' (II, 441). But equally, in Trollope's view, the Coalition fails because that is in the nature of coalitions; as he points out in his biography *Lord Palmerston* : 'Political coalitions are never firm because they are formed of individual men, and each man has a heart in his bosom in which he carries memories of the past as well as his hopes for the future.'[12] In the real political world partisan politics and personal ambition can never be suppressed for long.

During the many discussions of politics in the novel, a great deal of cant is talked about coalitions; how single party government is natural to English society and how coalitions are always feeble because they are based on compromised principles. It is certainly true that the Duke's administration is offensive to Mr Boffin's staunch, patriotic Conservatism and that the Radicals are disgusted at being led by such a mild man as Palliser, but as Trollope was well aware, the great majority of politicians simply resent sharing power. And the fundamental malaise of Victorian partisan politics is summarized in the way the old Duke regards the Coalition as a means of delaying reform, which results, as Mr Boffin complains, in a 'death-like torpor' (II, 3). However, politicians of both parties concur in approving of the way the Government has effectively stifled reformers like the Home Rulers, the economists and the philosophical Radicals and also approve of the way they share between themselves the spoils of office. Indeed, St Bungay himself admits that policies are only useful for creating a majority in the House. And like the old Duke, who also regards the Coalition as an essential device to buy time until another Liberal administration can be formed, all Trollope's politicians believe the regaining of party power to be of far greater importance than mere policies. This much is evident even to an observer like Mrs Finn, who recognizes that politics has nothing to do with reform and that there is never anything special to be done either by Conservatives or Liberals. There is genuine horror, therefore, when a Reform Bill, which has the support of the Prime Minister, is presented by the Coalition, and it is ironic that Mr Monk's county suffrage measure is finally lost by the development of a Liberal majority and the demise of the Coalition. But there is a much darker irony in Lady Glencora's shrewd assessment of political realities from the point of view of her own coterie: ' "I don't think it makes any difference as to what sort of laws are passed. But among ourselves, in our set, it makes a deal of difference who gets the garters, and the counties, who are made barons and then earls, and whose name stands at the head of everything" ' (I, 64).

Throughout *The Prime Minister* Trollope is concerned to demonstrate the opposing claims of politics as the focus of national aspirations and those of Realpolitik. And Palliser finds himself at the centre of this conflict. Almost alone among Trollope's politicians he is a statesman of genuine vision, who is also in touch with the realities of the workaday world outside the hothouse of politics. He can devote himself with equal delight to the extension of the franchise, decimal coinage, or to discussing the merits of cork soles. But ironically he is plainly unsuited to the Realpolitik of managing a *laisser-faire* Coalition.

He obstinately sets his face against short-term expedients and Trollope's revelation of his political creed fairly late in the novel does much to explain his sense of frustration at realizing the futility of power. His private vision feeds his misery at failing to define for himself 'the past policy of the last month or two' (I, 194). And against his colleagues' advice he supports Monk's bill as a small step along the road to democracy. Moreover, not only does Palliser lack the requisite charm, tact and thick skin to be an effective Prime Minister, but he continually allows moral values to get in the way of political decisions. By ignoring parliamentary traditions, like the appointment of the law officers of the Crown, by which he offends Sir Timothy Beeswax, and by his decision not to appease the powerful brewers' lobby, he inadvertently threatens the Coalition itself. And his political blunders accumulate. He snubs Sir Orlando Drought, refuses to interfere in the Silverbridge election, pays Lopez's election expenses and, most eccentric of all, he bestows a Garter on Lord Earlybird. Ignoring the advice of St Bungay – ' "You will offend all your own friends, and only incur the ridicule of your opponents" ' (II, 279) – Palliser believes that by acknowledging a meaningful relation between the Government, the aristocracy and the world of the ploughman he is giving public recognition to the concept of the nation as a community of interests. In the event, as his old mentor had predicted, he astonishes Lord Earlybird, disgusts his powerful supporter Lord Drummond and educates no one. Indeed, Palliser himself is unable to sustain the gesture, coming to feel like his colleagues that it is quixotic.

Apart from his scrupulosity and his love of virtue, Palliser's main political flaw is his innocence of the many-layered depths of cynicism around him. He is the unwitting tool of the old Duke, who regards him as a convenient patriotic symbol to hold the Coalition together in a way that a more nakedly political figure could not, and whose resignation, when the Government has run its course, will not damage a Liberal regrouping. A hard-headed realist, St Bungay treats politics with a curious mixture of patriotic devotion and frank cynicism, regarding it as a dignified but worthwhile game. And Trollope supplies the metaphor : 'As a man cuts in and out at a whist table, and enjoys both the game and the rest from the game, so had the Duke of St. Bungay been well pleased in either position' (II, 367). Long in political years and honours, the old Duke leaves the highest place to Palliser, not from natural diffidence, nor from aristocratic disdain, but quite simply because he does not want to surrender his real power as a king-maker. Similarly, the rest of Trollope's lesser politicians, like Phineas Finn, Sir Timothy Beeswax, Lord Drummond, or Barrington Erle, all respected figures, are so obsessed with power that they collectively sacrifice principles for place and pay in the Coalition, or alternatively use it as a springboard from which to launch a new ministry. This deep-rooted cynicism, shared by political wives like Mrs Finn and Glencora and so often masked by convincing political arguments and courteous eloquence – especially by the old Duke – constitutes one of Trollope's main criticisms of the political world. Contemporary politics, he felt, were partisan, static and ultimately sterile.

Trollope's view of Victorian politics, as revealed by the 'special case' which he examines, gains its effectiveness partly by being set against a densely realized background. He is very perceptive, for instance, about the many component parts that make up a coalition and how these agree with differing degrees of cohesion and cordiality. He details too the grasping of the good things of office, the in-fighting, the back-stairs intrigues, how opposition to the Coalition arises from the personal ambition of those who serve in it and the way politics is interwoven with social life. True power resides with a small coterie of Whig and Conservative aristocrats, and because Glencora instinctively realizes that for the Coalition to be a success political antagonists have to be bound by social rather than political ties she accordingly opens up Gatherum to the Government on a grand scale. Trollope also achieves a greater sense of realism by introducing a wider perspective. He makes us aware of the gulf that exists between what the newspaper-reading public is told and what the politicians themselves know about the daily health of the Government. And he reveals how the fragility of the Coalition can be laid embarrassingly bare by Glencora's tactless joke at one of her parties about the necessity for ministerial obedience.

Tolstoy was surely right in believing that in *The Prime Minister* Trollope had written a 'beautiful book'.[13] And his mastery lies not only in the breadth and maturity of his treatment of politics, his psychological insight and his social observation, but in his comprehensive grasp of the form of the novel. This is particularly in evidence as he develops the theme of coalition which articulates its different social, geographical and moral areas.[14] Trollope's characteristic formal techniques emphasize the way political life is shaped by personalities and individual experience is dominated by political instinct. At the beginning of Chapter IX, for instance, the focus moves from a discussion of the projected gatherings by means of which Glencora intends to cement the Coalition and gain a measure of real power for herself to the dinner-party given by the vulgar Mrs Roby, who has assembled an ill-assorted group of guests in order to enhance her own social prestige. Like Glencora she is using her unwilling husband, whose brother is in the Government, in order to extend her sphere of influence and enter the fashionable world. Moreover, she also employs the occasion to plot the coalition marriage of her niece Emily Wharton and Ferdinand Lopez. Like Glencora's parties, Mrs Roby's dinner is aimed at getting people to embrace publicly in a spirit of false harmony what they deplore in private, as Mr Roby, who detests his brother and Mr Wharton, who dislikes Lopez, have to do on this occasion. Indeed a further link with the world of the Pallisers is made by the subject of dinner-table conversation. Here in private Mr Roby, a party whip and a thoroughly professional politician, reveals the true nature of the Duke's patriotic Government and corroborates the insights offered by Mrs Finn and Glencora : ' "The truth is" he says, "there's nothing special to be done at the present moment, and there's no reason why we shouldn't agree and divide the good things between us" ' (I, 104).

This small-scale local articulation of one of the novel's main themes forms part of a much larger emblematic pattern. Glencora's great parties at Gatherum, which represent the Coalition in the popular mind, also find their private counterpart in

Lopez's dinner-party at his father-in-law's house in Manchester Square. Just as at Glencora's gatherings, which Palliser describes with some force as vulgar, there is a loose association of politicians, parasites, bores and hangers-on, so Lopez has recruited to his dinner-table a bunch of disreputable people who might be useful to him. Both Glencora and Lopez are encouraged by the sheer scope of their ambition to replace true hospitality with utilitarian, professional catering in houses that have never been home to them. While Glencora pursues reputation and power, Lopez strives for money and influence. In each case the voice of conscience is present but unheeded, for just as Palliser turns up unexpectedly at Gatherum and expresses his censure, Mr Wharton appears, like Banquo's ghost, halfway through the Lopez banquet to the consternation of his guests. What these gatherings reveal, like the structure and machinery of the Government itself, is that all attempts at coalition are concerned basically with reducing people to objects of political will. Consequently they are tasteless, joyless and divisive, and serve only to lay bare the atomistic social relations which it is their overt purpose to conceal beneath a spurious, temporary unity.

Trollope's development of his moral vision by means of counterpoint extends to his treatment of the middle classes in the large balancing mass of the novel. His criticism of the political world as being in-bred and based on aristocratic patronage is equally applicable to the powerful landed classes. Just as Glencora thinks of the old Duke as a king-maker and her husband as a surrogate king, John Fletcher is known to his family as 'king John'. They too are autocratic and insular, living in rural kingdoms on the Welsh border run on almost feudal lines. What Trollope draws attention to by these parallels is the division of power between the political world of London and the gentry of the shires. It is an arrangement which suits both groups. They respect each other's claims to power and each is content to leave the other alone. But the parallels between them are closer even than this, for like the Coalition Government, the Wharton–Fletcher alliance has been formed primarily to protect class interests. Although, like Sir Alured Wharton, the Fletchers feel that their traditional obligation to the local community requires that they should lose a little money on their farming, it is a moral luxury that they can afford only because their real wealth is made elsewhere. In fact it is founded on those very politics of coalition which they overtly abhor. It comes from marriages, like the projected match between Arthur Fletcher and Emily Wharton, where Mr Wharton's £60,000, made from a lifetime's work as a commercial lawyer is to be added to the Fletchers' acres in a union of money and land. Indeed, the whole existence of the landed classes, Trollope suggests, is underwritten by the continued coalition with city cash, an uncomfortable truth that provokes their uneasy, defensive sneers at city wealth and city life. But this coalition also shares another significant feature with the public world of Westminster politics. It is only a temporary hiatus between single-party governments. The Fletchers are content to absorb Wharton money so that the Whartons also become in time an extension of the Fletcher party, which is the eventual outcome of the courtship of Arthur and Emily. This political instinct, developed over centuries of acquisition, and which binds families into one 'party' is, as Glencora recognizes, what makes them impregnable.

As the world goes the Whartons and Fletchers are the bedrock of society – sober, sensible, useful and even kindly people. But their political solidarity of an almost tribal kind represents a fundamental narrowness of heart, a resistance to change and a denial of any sense of national community. And when their partisanship is manifested through prejudice it can be morally vicious and destructive. They admit with some pride that they are prejudiced people, meaning by this their possession of an instinctive moral rectitude, an old-fashioned standard of gentlemanly conduct which is the fountainhead of honour and a guarantee of the rightness of their social position. But in truth it is a sure political instinct which enables them to embrace, without any sense of guilt, a cynical and utilitarian view of humanity. Their morality is fully tested by their treatment of Emily Wharton and Lopez. Their overt judgement of Lopez is made in terms of his foreignness and his relative poverty. And he is doubly marked as an outsider because he is neither sufficiently wealthy nor secure enough socially to cultivate prejudices of his own. But what really outrages them is his opposition to the Wharton-Fletcher alliance and he is quickly identified as a political enemy. Political to their fingertips, the Fletchers drop Emily immediately upon her marriage, ostensibly because she has disgraced herself, but in truth because they resent Lopez's success in winning her over to the opposition. And in formal terms Trollope tactfully reinforces this point by the electoral contest between Lopez and Arthur Fletcher at Silverbridge, which makes a parallel with their equally political battle for Emily's allegiance. However, since after Lopez's death Emily's money is still intact, it becomes expedient to welcome her back into the party. After a long debate the Fletchers decide on a policy of forgiveness; they manipulate her emotions unashamedly at her brother's wedding until she acquiesces finally in marrying Arthur Fletcher, something, ironically, that she had long set her heart on, having repented her excursion into the wilderness.

In his treatment of the personal lives of the middle classes Trollope mirrors unerringly the ruling principles of the larger political world. Striving for power, they survive on covert coalitions which they are ashamed to acknowledge publicly and which for the most part they conceal successfully even from themselves. As in the larger world the overwhelming reason why Lopez is resented, snubbed and excluded is that his ambitions come to symbolize for his social enemies the possibility of a genuine coalition between the different classes, between the establishment and outsiders and between the spheres of finance and politics. This is an anathema to people like the Whartons and the Fletchers for it represents a possible movement towards a more open and dynamic society and a permanent shift in the whole balance of social power. They bulk large in the novel precisely because their rigidity, inertia and partisan politics are symptomatic of the paralysis that Trollope felt was gripping English life.

The middle classes fear not only what Lopez symbolizes but also his obvious political gifts, for he is all political instinct. Significantly, we first encounter him at the Liberal Reform Club where he curries favour with Everett Wharton. Then he uses

Emily's aunt to gain access to her, plays on his heroism in rescuing Everett from the thieves, trades on Mr Wharton's loneliness and exploits his business partner Sexty Parker's greed. Thick-skinned, sharp-witted, charming and plausible, Lopez fastens on people's weaknesses and exploits them remorselessly. For him every meeting is a political event, each encounter with his father-in-law is a series of careful manoeuvres for advantage, and it is a measure of his political acumen that he manages to ingratiate himself with Glencora and gain entry to the great world of Gatherum. But Trollope is concerned to present a balanced view of Lopez. He is so utterly devoid of principles, Trollope tells us, as to be almost an innocent, who 'had no inner appreciation whatsoever of what was really good or what was really bad in a man's conduct' (II, 203). More importantly, Trollope makes it clear that his complete lack of moral values is simply irrelevant to the kind of judgements made of him by the Wharton–Fletcher clan, whose own mode of behaviour, like his, is rooted in political expediency; and Trollope makes a careful parallel between Lopez's cynical manipulation of people and that of the irreproachable figures like the old Duke, Glencora and the Fletchers. Lopez is hated because he lives as the world lives, not as it pretends to live. Trollope's measured sympathy for him becomes increasingly evident in those interior views that we are given of him shortly before his suicide, in which we are made aware of his genuine love for his wife and his sorrow at the ruin of Sexty Parker and his family. But although Lopez is a predator, Trollope affirms that in a real sense he is also society's victim. That other thorough politician, Glencora, who is deeply implicated in his unfortunate career, knows only too well how society musters its forces against the outsider and she is honest enough to share the blame, as she remarks to Mrs Finn: ' "I have a sort of feeling, you know, that among us we made the train run over him" ' (II, 425).

In this chillingly pessimistic study of the tyranny, the gradations and the limitations of power, Trollope's placing of Lopez's attempt to enter Parliament at the formal and moral centre of the novel is of greater significance, in my view, than critics have recognized. By this means Trollope suggests the possibility of the kind of coalition which he feels to be necessary, acknowledges how ambiguous it must necessarily be, and how it is inevitably denied. Although Lopez wants a seat in the House in order to advance his career, in the real, tainted world modern men like him who have drive and energy even though their personal morality is dubious, are needed as desperately as people like Palliser, who have a larger vision, who recognize the existence of the real world and are prepared to govern it. It is this utterly unlikely coalition of political idealism and self-help which the political world requires in order to rediscover its energy and sense of direction. But, such is Trollope's deliberately ironic use of the 'special case' that both Palliser and Lopez are badly flawed symbols. His ideal statesman is too honourable and scrupulous to dirty his hands and become an effective politician, while the dynamic new man is too innately corrupt to be able to envisage the national interest.

Nevertheless, the Silverbridge election, I think, offers the novel's central statement, although it does so equivocally. And several personal and political relations hinge on its outcome, giving it a dramatic as well as an emblematic significance – Emily's marriage, Glencora's reputation and influence, Palliser's integrity, as well as Lopez's career. But the possibility of the emergence of a new political style based on this kind of symbolic coalition between the Liberal Prime Minister and the foreign interloper founders precisely because it is at this point in the novel that its two plots converge with complex and telling effect. It is part of both Trollope's moral design and his social criticism that Lopez is offered and fails to gain the one seat in England that seems certain, and that he is refused the dowry he has every right to expect. In both cases, trying to emulate the English, he relies mistakenly on their tradition of fair play, but is defeated by politics masquerading as morality. Mr Wharton, whose social and racial prejudice is extreme, reneges on his moral obligation, ostensibly to protect his daughter, but really in order to retain power over Lopez's actions. And by doing so he confirms Lopez's role as an outcast and contributes to his estrangement from Emily and to his eventual suicide. Palliser's reaction to Lopez's candidacy is similarly governed by a confusion of motives. His resistance to Glencora's interference in the election has as much to do with their political rivalry as it has to do with the issue of electoral purity. Although he feels that he must endorse reform, his action, as the Duchess well knows, runs counter to tradition and is rank bad politics. Moreover, his decision is also morally dubious because it stems partly from a growing intoxication with public displays of virtue. The profound irony of this central episode in the novel is that the possibility for advancing Trollope's liberal ideal of bringing closer together the different classes, the worlds of work and of politics, the qualities of vision and dynamism, idealism and political skill, founder on the rocks of prejudice, pride and political naïvety. It reveals not only Trollope's mature breadth of political vision, but also the depths of his pessimism, as English political and social life fail so comprehensively.

Like Anna in *Anna Karenina*, whose suicide his resembles, Lopez feels keenly the defeat of his attempt to enter society on its own terms. And since, as an outsider, he equates success with social acceptance and advancement, he finally bows to its assessment of his worthlessness and kills himself with the same appalling logic as does Melmotte. And Lopez's choice of Tenway Junction for his suicide is also a significant aspect of Trollope's social criticism. It makes a daring counterpoint late in the novel with the great world of Gatherum as Lopez returns from the drawing-rooms of polite society to die in the workaday world. These milieux are symbolic of the social extremes of the Victorian age. They present more than simply a contrast between Government and governed, rich and poor; they symbolize the gulf between past and present. Gatherum, the elegant home of the Whig coterie, is the symbol of an era that has outlived its usefulness. Tenway Junction, by contrast, is a potent symbol of an industrial age, propelled by the impersonal forces of change, which the aristocracy and the middle classes strive to resist. Its emergence as an important symbol late in the novel serves to place in perspective all the preceding political discussion. Essentially, Trollope is employing a reductive process, for from this point of view all the politics in *The Prime Minister* are seen as little more than manoeuvrings in a vacuum, quite unrelated to the larger modern society that has to be governed.

Politics dominates the world of *The Prime Minister* not only in terms of its larger themes, but also in the area of intimate personal relations, for here too people inevitably become objects of another's will. This is one aspect of the surprising parallels which Trollope draws between Glencora and Lopez, who tries to rule Mr Wharton through his wife Emily. Similarly, Glencora, who is admired by that professional politician, Barrington Erle, because she is totally lacking in scruples, manipulates her husband in order to strengthen her political influence. And this is brought out in her conversation with Lopez about the Silverbridge candidacy: 'She certainly had a little syllogism in her head as to the Duke ruling the borough, the Duke's wife ruling the Duke, and therefore the Duke's wife ruling the borough' (I, 237). And what goes for the borough goes for the country as well. Indeed, in every area of life we find people being constrained to act in a political way. Like Lopez, they are always 'in the inner workings of their minds, defending themselves and attacking others' (I, 5), a process which produces façades and evasions of truth and turns meetings into encounters which alter the balance of political forces in personal relations. And nowhere is this more evident than in Trollope's superbly subtle study of the uneasy coalition marriage of Glencora and Plantagenet Palliser, a marriage threatened by political rivalry, because their private relationship is thoroughly interwoven with politics. Discovering that neither tenderness nor respect can replace the innate sympathy necessary for a harmonious life, they are always fighting against each other, Palliser because he shrewdly suspects that the old Duke selected him for his wife's gregariousness and utilitarianism, and because her popularity reduces his political stature; Glencora because she is desperately competing with her husband and subconsciously working for his fall. She in particular is acutely conscious of the irony of their roles for, as she tells Mrs Finn: ' "They should have made me Prime Minister, and have let him be Chancellor of the Exchequer. I begin to see the ways of Government now. I could have done all the dirty work" ' (II, 186). And she sets up her own rival 'cabinet' with Mrs Finn, which becomes a symbol of her covert battle with her husband for political supremacy that lasts throughout the novel. This situation breeds a feeling of insecurity in Palliser and he is driven to assert his authority through 'unpolitical', subversive actions which will shake the Coalition while leaving him morally impregnable. His quixotic gift of the Garter, for instance, is a consciously statesmanlike act, but it also serves to assure him of his possession of authority and, more importantly, draws attention away from his wife. Yet, paradoxically, he is increasingly unhappy as Prime Minister and wishes the Coalition could be brought to an honourable conclusion. Trollope succeeds with splendid psychological realism in showing Palliser desperately striving to reconcile these tensions, which arise out of the politics of marriage, in a way that will be seen neither by the public world nor by his own conscience as in any way dishonourable.

However, what people fear most in political life, Trollope reveals, is not conflict or compromise but the corollary of ambition – failure. This is what Palliser, especially, dreads and Trollope points out that this is why people like him cling to power long after it has ceased to be rewarding (I, 304). Because, as Palliser admits to Phineas Finn in an unguarded moment, he is only truly alive when he is immersed in political activity, he equates political defeat with personal inadequacy. It is the complex tensions that this engenders, rather than the corrupting effect of power, that lead him to grow imperious, comparing himself, when he has finally lost office, to Caesar who cannot consent to serve under Pompey. It is a triumph of Trollope's astute characterization that his Prime Minister is so morally alert that he is profoundly aware and ashamed of this process in himself, but like his jealousy of his wife it is something he finds himself powerless to alter. Of course Glencora, too, fears failure, but in her case it stems from her sense of her inadequacy as a woman. Since her marriage is unfulfilling, she puts all her emotional capital into her political schemes and she cannot bear the feeling of personal defeat that accompanies the collapse of her grand parties. She realizes with shame her lack of the dignity required of a truly great lady and that her endeavours have been slightly ridiculous. And Lopez, whose career makes a strong parallel with Palliser and Glencora, also fears public failure more than anything, even death. However, inexorably, and in Trollope's view inevitably, all the coalitions in the novel, matrimonial, social and political, end in shame and a bitter sense of defeat, creating in the process a formal pattern which helps to chart its underlying political rhythms.

In addition to the dread of failure, what all the characters share in this thoroughly political book, is the profound sense of living in a much ampler world than that of ordinary people. Palliser indeed finds the floodlit stage unnerving, feeling that both he and his administration are being judged against the backcloth of history, while Glencora urgently seeks her place in history too (I, 321). This awareness of the drama of political life is further developed by Trollope's intercalation into the novel at several important points pertinent references to Shakespeare. Lopez, for instance, describes himself to Mr Wharton as a romantic Shakespearean merchant, believing that he inhabits a sphere of heroic entrepreneurship in which petty morality does not apply. To Sexty Parker on another occasion he calls himself a Shylock in business, which serves to emphasize his role as the focus of racial prejudice. Like Shylock he is a rather ambiguous social victim, tricked by a middle class lawyer of irreproachable background. However, Mr Wharton's racial disgust and covert hatred emerge as he violently compares himself to Brabantio whose daughter has been stolen from him by a black, and when he echoes Hamlet's morbid distinction between his father (Hyperion–Fletcher) and Claudius (a satyr–Lopez). And in a novel which, as I discussed in an earlier chapter, draws on Fletcher's *Women Pleased* and in which John Fletcher uses the early drama to furnish a moral guide for his brother (I, 179), it should not surprise us to discover not only references to *The Merchant of Venice*, *Othello* and *Hamlet*, but also to *Macbeth*, *King Lear* and *Coriolanus*, a play which anticipates some of the political themes of *The Prime Minister*. Trollope employs these references both as a way of indicating his characters' acute self-knowledge and of registering their sense of living in a world that is much larger than life. Palliser compares himself with

Coriolanus, the high-minded hero who will not bend to the vulgar for approval, and Glencora sees her situation mirrored in that of Lady Macbeth. She acknowledges the workings of fate, testifies to her husband's high integrity, but at the same time recognizes her innate ambition and her powerful influence over his actions. Similarly, when Palliser refuses to nominate a candidate for Silverbridge she likens him to Lear foolishly surrendering power, and near the conclusion of the novel she compares him sadly to Othello whose occupation has now gone. These various postures which the characters strike echo the Shakespearean tragic themes of family feuding, political conflicts, racial hatred and revenge, and in a cumulative way they serve to emphasize the lust for power and the reduction of people to instruments of political will which, for all its superficial decorum and urbanity, The Prime Minister is really concerned with.

Finally, however, an important function of these Shakespearean echoes is that of ironic reduction. They form a contrast from the point of high art, of genuine political action, of real tragic significance, by which we are enabled to judge the smallness of the world of The Prime Minister. We recognize the ultimately inconsequential nature of its politics and the inability of its people to reach the heights of energy, will and passionate commitment of the Shakespearean figures, or to be imbued as they are with a sense of destiny. Trollope's superbly artistic employment of these subtle parallels not only draws attention to the fine low-key realism of his mimetic art, but it also offers his telling judgement on the moral stature of the Victorian world.

NOTES

I INTRODUCTION

1 C. P. Snow, 'Trollope: The Psychological Stream', in *On the Novel* ed. B. S. Benedikz (London, 1971), p. 3.
2 James R. Kincaid, 'Bring Back *The Trollopian*', *Nineteenth Century Fiction*, 31 (1976), p. 5.
3 R. C. Terry, *Anthony Trollope: The Artist in Hiding* (London, 1977), p. 54.
4 Frederick Locker-Lampson, *My Confidences, An Autobiographical Sketch* (London, 1896), p. 331.
5 *An Autobiography*, p. 314.
6 *An Autobiography*, p. 310.
7 *An Autobiography*, p. 136.
8 Frederic Harrison, 'Anthony Trollope', *Macmillan's Magazine*, XLIX (Nov. 1883), p. 54; *Studies in Early Victorian Literature* (London, 1895), p. 203.
9 *An Autobiography*, p. 120.
10 T. H. S. Escott, 'Anthony Trollope, An Appreciation and Reminiscence', *Fortnightly Review*, LXXX (Dec. 1906), p. 1102.
11 *Thackeray*, p. 169.
12 *Thackeray*, p. 122.
13 *An Autobiography*, p. 274.
14 *An Autobiography*, p. 120.
15 *Letters*. p. 217.
16 *Thackeray*, p. 185.
17 *Thackeray*, p. 186.
18 S. W. Dawson, *Drama and the Dramatic* (London, 1970), p. 79.
19 See George Eliot, 'Leaves from a Note-Book', in *Essays*, ed. C. L. Lewes (London, 1884), p. 358; Trollope, *An Autobiography*, pp. 126, 190.
20 George Saintsbury, *Corrected Impressions* (London, 1895), p. 175.
21 Kenneth Graham, *English Criticism of the Novel 1865–1900* (Oxford, 1965), p. 21.
22 David Skilton, *Anthony Trollope and his con-*

temporaries (London, 1972).

23 See Victoria and Albert Museum Library, Forster Collection, F.S. 8vo 8968, Trollope; Catalogue of His Books (London, 1874); see also *Marginalia*.

24 F. E. Trollope, *Frances Trollope: Her Life and Literary Work* (London, 1895), vol. I, 89–90, and T. A. Trollope, *What I Remember* (London, 1887), vol. I, 180–1.

25 F. E. Trollope, *Frances Trollope*, vol. I, 246–7.

26 T. A. Trollope, *What I Remember*, vol. I, 25.

27 A. G. L'Estrange, ed., *The Friendships of Mary Russell Mitford* (London, 1882), vol. I, 160, 228, 239.

28 Anthony Trollope, 'George Henry Lewes', *Fortnightly Review*, n.s. XXV (1879), pp. 15–24, and *Letters*, p. 252. Many of Lewes's critical notices were collected and published in *On Actors*

and the Art of Acting (London, 1875) at Trollope's suggestion, and the volume is prefaced (pp. v–xii) by an 'Epistle to Anthony Trollope'.

29 W. C. Roscoe, 'De Foe as a Novelist', *National Review*, III (1856), pp. 380–2.

30 T. H. S. Escott, *Anthony Trollope: His Work, Associates and Literary Originals* (London, 1913), p. 142, and Henry Taylor, *Correspondence*, ed. E. Dowden (London, 1888), p. 75.

31 Escott, *Anthony Trollope: His Work, Associates and Literary Originals*, p. 182.

32 *An Autobiography*, p. 253.

33 See especially Asa Briggs, 'Trollope, Bagehot and the English Constitution', *Cambridge Journal*, V (1952), pp. 327–38.

34 C. J. Vincent, 'Trollope : A Victorian Augustan', *Queen's Quarterly*, LII (1945), pp. 415–27.

II TROLLOPE AND THE DRAMA

1 *An Autobiography*, p. 100.

2 *An Autobiography*, p. 315.

3 Bradford A. Booth, 'Trollope's *Orley Farm*: Artistry *Manqué*', in *From Jane Austen to Joseph Conrad*, ed. R. C. Rathburn and M. Steinmann. (Minneapolis, 1958), pp. 153–5.

4 Ruth apRoberts refers to Bradford A. Booth's discoveries in her study, *Trollope: Artist and Moralist* (London, 1971), and A. O. J. Cockshut notes Trollope's more general affinity with the early dramatists in *Anthony Trollope: A Critical Study* (London, 1955).

5 John H. Hagan, 'The Divided Mind of Anthony Trollope', *Nineteenth Century Fiction*, 14 (1959), pp. 1–26.

6 *The Dramatic Works of Sir William D'Avenant*, ed. J. Maidment and W. H. Logan, 5 vols (London, 1873), vol. IV, 131.

7 Trollope writes that had he given himself a fair chance, 'by continued labour [Middleton] might have excelled all the Elizabethan dramatists except Shakespeare', *Marginalia*, PR2711 D8 As. Col., *The Works of Thomas Middleton*, ed. A. Dyce, 5 vols (London, 1840), vol. IV, 635. Charles Reade recognized the innately dramatic quality of *Ralph the Heir* and drew heavily on it in his play *Shilly-Shally*.

8 What convinced Trollope of the novel's merit was his readers' horror at the social heresy it proclaimed, see *An Autobiography*, p. 298.

9 *Letters*, p. 308.

10 Trollope thought the play 'obscure', although he admired the moral tone of Ford's work, see *Marginalia*, PR2521 G5 1869 As. Col., *The Works of John Ford*, ed. W. Gifford, revised A. Dyce, 3 vols (London, 1869), vol. II, 321.

11 Trollope's work sheets indicate his concern with the precise formulation of the Earl's claim, which he had checked by a lawyer friend, and they demonstrate Trollope's assessment of its importance in the novel, see *Papers*, MS. Don. C.10., p. 7.

12 Quoted in Bradford A. Booth, *Anthony Trollope: Aspects of His Life and Art* (London, 1958), p. 129. Trollope read *The Old Law* in 1876, see *Marginalia*, PR2711 D8 As. Col., *The Works of Thomas Middleton*, ed. A. Dyce, 5 vols (London, 1840), vol. I, 120.

13 *Marginalia*, PR2421 D8 1843 As. Col., *The Works of Beaumont and Fletcher*, ed. A. Dyce, 11 vols (London, 1843–6), vol. VII, 94. As Inga-Stina Ewbank has pointed out in 'Anthony Trollope's Copy of the 1647 Beaumont and Fletcher Folio', *Notes and Queries*, 204 (1959), 153–5, this copy is in the library of the Shakespeare Institute. From his marginalia dating in this edition it is evident that for some reason *Women Pleased* was one of only a few Fletcher plays which Trollope omitted to read during his first period of study in the Renaissance and Jacobean drama in the years 1850 to 1853.

14 There are other echoes in *The Prime Minister* of the names of characters in *Women Pleased*: Silvio's aunt is named Rhodope, while Emily's aunt is called Roby, and the name of Emily's lover, Arthur Fletcher, may be an unconscious echo of that of the play's author.

15 W. P. Ker, 'Anthony Trollope', in *On Modern Literature*, ed. T. Spencer and J. Sutherland (Oxford, 1955), p. 146.

16 *Marginalia*, PR1263 D6 As. Col., *A Select Collection of Old English Plays*, ed. R. Dodsley, 12 vols (London, 1825–7), vol. VI, 202; *The Works of Beaumont and Fletcher*, ed. A. Dyce vol. VI, 538–9, vol. VIII, 324.

17 Anthony Trollope, 'Henry Taylor's Poems', *Fortnightly Review*, I (1865), p. 130.

18 Anthony Trollope, 'A Walk in a Wood', *Good Words*, XX (1879), p. 600.

19 Trollope,'A Walk in a Wood', p. 600.

20 Trollope, 'A Walk in a Wood', p. 597.

21 G. G. Sedgewick, *Of Irony, Especially in Drama*, (Toronto, 1948), p. 32.

22 *Papers*, MS. Don. C.10., pp. 15–21. Trollope's planning of a scenario for *The Way We Live Now* is particularly interesting because it clearly indicates his original intention to put Melmotte on trial for forgery instead of having him commit suicide. See P. D. Edwards, 'Trollope Changes His Mind : The Death of Melmotte in *The Way We Live Now*', *Nineteenth Century Fiction* 18 (1963), pp. 89–91.

III THE FORM OF THE STORY

1 Jerome Thale, 'The Problem of Structure in Trollope', *Nineteenth Century Fiction*, 15 (1960), p. 147.

2 Thale, in *Nineteenth Century Fiction*, 15, p. 149.

3 Ruth apRoberts, *Trollope: Artist and Moralist*, (London, 1971), p. 39. She regards the multi-plotted novels as 'elaborations of this unit' (p. 48), but in my view this underestimates their dynamic quality.

4 *An Autobiography*, p. 205.

5 Trollope continually defends this practice, in the concluding chapter of an early novel like *The Three Clerks* and at greater length in Chapter 35 of *The Eustace Diamonds*.

6 See Mario Praz, *The Hero in Eclipse in Victorian Fiction*,

trans. Angus Davidson
(London, 1956).

7 Ruth apRoberts has an interesting discussion of this aspect of Mr Crawley's character in *Trollope: Artist and Moralist*, p. 104.

8 Juliet McMaster in her article, ' "The Unfortunate Moth": Unifying Theme in *The Small House at Allington*', *Nineteenth Century Fiction*, 26 (1971), pp. 127–44, argues persuasively that there is a strong element of masochism in the relation between Lily Dale and John Eames in *The Small House at Allington* and *The Last Chronicle of Barset*.

9 She argues that they 'display and define the Trollopian unit of structure', *Trollope: Artist and Moralist*, p. 46.

10 An exception is William A. West, 'The Anonymous Trollope', ARIEL, 5 (1974), pp. 46–64, which makes an interesting general assessment of these novels.

11 *An Autobiography*, p. 175.

12 R. C. Terry, *Anthony Trollope: The Artist in Hiding* (London, 1977), p. 37.

13 Richard Stang, *The Theory of the Novel in England 1850–1870* (London, 1959), p. 122. Stang noted that

Trollope's friend Henry Taylor also favoured the intensively dramatic novel.

14 G. H. Lewes, 'Realism in Art: Recent German Fiction', *Westminster Review*, LXX (1858), p. 496.

15 This is probably the reason for Trollope's high regard for this novel, which he considered to be better even than his much more popular work, *The Eustace Diamonds*, see *An Autobiography*, p. 296.

16 R. H. Hutton, who admired *Nina Balatka* and who immediately identified its author, points to this scene as the moral centre of the novel, see Smalley, *Critical Heritage*, p. 269. He also shared Lewes's and Trollope's concern with the 'Ideal' in fiction. For a fuller discussion of Hutton as a critic of Trollope see David Skilton, *Anthony Trollope and his contemporaries* (London, 1972).

17 It is significant that Trollope's later recollection of this novel was that it ended 'unhappily', *Letters*, pp. 282–3.

18 Donald Smalley ed., *Anthony Trollope: The Critical Heritage* (London, 1969) pp. 445–8.

IV THE RHETORICAL DESIGN

1 See, for instance, 'British Novelists – Richardson, Miss Austen, Scott', *Fraser's Magazine*, LXI (1860), p. 21.

2 Smalley, *Critical Heritage*, p. 209.

3 Henry James, *Partial Portraits* (London, 1919), p. 116.

4 This debate was sharply focused by Robert Scholes and Robert Kellogg in *The Nature of Narrative* (London, 1966), where they argue the case for the novelist as creator rather than as *histor*.

5 James, *Partial Portraits*, p. 103.

6 James, *Partial Portraits*, p. 116.

7 Trollope's wide knowledge is revealed in his *London Tradesmen*, ed. Michael Sadleir (London, 1927), pp. 12–22.

8 See Richard Stang, *The Theory of the Novel in England 1850–1870* (London, 1959), pp. 48–51.

9 *An Autobiography*, p. 126.

10 *An Autobiography*, p. 186.

11 *An Autobiography*, p. 190.

12 Ruth apRoberts, *Trollope: Artist and Moralist* (London, 1971), p. 52.

13 See Trollope's *The Three Clerks*, in which Charley Tudor's editor "specially insists on a Nemesis", p. 214.

14 *Thackeray*, p. 201.

15 *Letters*, p. 218.

16 They were later collected and published under the title *Caxtoniana* (London, 1875).

17 Compare Edward Bulwer-Lytton, 'On Certain Principles of Art in Works of Imagination', *Blackwood's Edinburgh Magazine*, XCIII (1863), p. 552 with Trollope, 'On English Prose Fiction as a Rational Amusement', in *Four Lectures*, ed. M. L. Parrish (London, 1938), p. 124.

18 Trollope, *Four Lectures*, p. 124.

19 Compare *An Autobiography*, pp. 199–200 with Edward Bulwer-Lytton, 'The Sympathetic Temperament', *Blackwood's Edinburgh Magazine*, XCII (1862), pp. 540–1.

20 Edward Bulwer-Lytton, 'On Art in Fiction', *Pamphlets and Sketches* (London, 1875), p. 352. This article first appeared anonymously in the first volume of the *Monthly Chronicle* in 1838 under the title 'The Critic'.

21 *An Autobiography*, p. 200.

22 Bradford A. Booth, 'Trollope's *Orley Farm*: Artistry Manqué', in *From Jane Austen to Joseph Conrad*, ed. R. C. Rathburn and M. Steinmann (Minneapolis,

1958), pp. 146–59.

23 Robert M. Adams, 'Orley Farm and Real Fiction', *Nineteenth Century Fiction*, 8 (1953), p. 37.

24 Robert M. Polhemus, *The Changing World of Anthony Trollope* (Berkeley and Los Angeles, 1968), p. 79.

25 As Trollope makes clear, although a 'trial' novel, *Orley Farm* is not concerned with arousing suspense, and his insistence on this point may have been an attempt to dissociate it from the sensationalism of such contemporary successes as Miss Braddon's *Lady Audley's Secret*.

26 The parallel from Molière is between Felix Graham and Arnolphe who, fearing he will be cuckolded, has a peasant's daughter Agnès brought up in complete ignorance of the world. While he is absent Agnès meets and falls in love with Horace, just as Mary Snow does with Albert Fitzallen. Both the play and the novel show how human nature cannot be circumvented by strategy. See also Bradford A. Booth, in *From Jane Austen to Joseph Conrad*, pp. 153–5.

27 George Saintsbury also makes this point in *Corrected Impressions* (London, 1895), p. 172.

28 *The Letters and Private Papers of W. M. Thackeray*, ed. G. N. Ray (London, 1946), vol. IV, 236.

29 See Kathleen Tillotson, *Novels of the Eighteen-Forties* (Oxford, 1954), p. 29.

30 *An Autobiography*, p. 236. See also Michael Sadleir, *Trollope: A Bibliography* (London, 1928, repr. 1964), p. 78.

31 *Papers*, MS. Don. C.10., pp. 24–5.

32 *Papers*, MS. Don. C.9., pp. 72–3, pp. 125–6, pp. 146–7.

33 *Papers*, MS. Don. C.9., p. 146.

34 *Papers*, MS. Don. C.9., p. 142.

35 *Letters*, p. 137.

36 *Letters*, p. 458.

37 *An Autobiography*, pp. 120–1.

38 *An Autobiography*, p. 120.

39 *Thackeray*, p. 38.

40 *Thackeray*, p. 95.

41 *Thackeray*, p. 201.

42 Smalley, *Critical Heritage*, p. 133.

43 Dickens experienced difficulty with Mrs Gaskell over the publication of *North and South* in 1855, and the manuscript of *Wives and Daughters* shows why Dickens had the editorial labour that he did, for, written on large sides of paper, the story goes on without a break even for

chapter divisions; see John
Rylands Library, English

MS. 877, Wives and
Daughters (c. 1864–6), 920 ff.

V THE ACHIEVEMENT

1 Smalley, *Critical Heritage*,
p. 401.

2 *An Autobiography*, p. 305.

3 James R. Kincaid, *The
Novels of Anthony Trollope*
(Oxford, 1977), pp. 164–5.

4 There are several similarities
between Melmotte and
Dickens's Merdle, although
the precise nature of
Trollope's debt is by no
means clear: 'According to
Escott, Trollope denied the
possibility of his having
been influenced by Dickens,
saying, "*The Way We Live
Now* appeared in 1875; I
only read *Little Dorrit* on my
way to Germany in 1878".
Now, somebody is mistaken
here; for Trollope not only
read *Little Dorrit* in the
monthly numbers as it
appeared (1856–7), but he
wrote an article on it!'
Bradford A. Booth, 'Trollope
and *Little Dorrit*', *Nineteenth
Century Fiction*, 2 (1947), p.
237.

5 Quoted in Michael Sadleir,
Trollope: A Commentary
(London, 1961 edn.) p. 426.

6 Smalley, *Critical Heritage*, p.
426.

7 *An Autobiography*, pp.
250–1, 253.

8 See Asa Briggs, 'Trollope,
Bagehot and the English
Constitution', *Cambridge
Journal*, V (1952), pp. 327–38.

9 *An Autobiography*, p. 253.

10 See Bradford A. Booth,
*Anthony Trollope: Aspects of
His Life and Art* (London,
1958), pp. 99 and 101; Robert
Polhemus, *The Changing
World of Anthony Trollope*
(Berkeley and Los Angeles,
1968), p. 208; Ruth apRoberts,
Trollope: Artist and Moralist
(London, 1971), pp. 145–6;
and John Halperin, *Trollope
and Politics* (London, 1977),
p. 222.

11 *An Autobiography*, pp. 308–9.

12 Anthony Trollope, *Lord
Palmerston* (London 1882),
p. 163.

13 N. N. Glisev, *Chronicle of
the Life and Work of L. N.
Tolstoy 1818–1890* (Moscow,
1958), p. 315.

14 Robert Polhemus makes this
point (in *The Changing
World of Anthony Trollope*,
p. 198).

SELECT BIBLIOGRAPHY

This is primarily a selected list of works which I have found useful in writing this study. I have kept it reasonably concise because both James R. Kincaid, in *The Novels of Anthony Trollope* (Oxford, 1977) and R. C. Terry, in *Anthony Trollope: The Artist in Hiding* (London, 1977) have included fairly comprehensive bibliographies of general works on Trollope, while David Skilton, in *Anthony Trollope and His Contemporaries*, (London, 1972) and Donald Smalley, in *Trollope: The Critical Heritage* (London, 1969) have published extensive selections of Victorian reviews and criticism. Specific editions of texts and other documents by Trollope are given in the Note on References, p. x.

BIBLIOGRAPHIES

Helling, Rafael, *A Century of Trollope Criticism* (Helsinki, 1956).

Irwin, Mary L., *Anthony Trollope: A Bibliography* (New York, 1926).

Ray, Gordon N., *Bibliographical Resources for the Study of Nineteenth Century English Fiction* (Los Angeles, 1964).

Sadleir, Michael, *Trollope: A Bibliography*, (London, 1928, supplemented 1934, reprinted London, 1964).

Sadleir, Michael, *Nineteenth Century Fiction, A Bibliographical Record*, 2 vols (London, 1951).

Smalley, Donald, 'Anthony Trollope', *Victorian Fiction: A Guide to Research*, ed. Lionel Stevenson (Cambridge, Mass., 1964).

Smalley, Donald, ed., *Trollope: The Critical Heritage* (London, 1969).

GENERAL WORKS ON TROLLOPE

Banks, J. A., 'The Way They Lived Then: Anthony Trollope and the 1870's', *Victorian Studies*, 12 (1968), 177–200.

Booth, Bradford A., *Anthony Trollope: Aspects of His Life and Art* (London, 1958).

Booth, Bradford A., 'Trollope on the Novel', *Essays Critical and Historical Dedicated to Lily B. Campbell* (Berkeley and Los Angeles, 1950), pp. 219–31.

Booth, Bradford, A., ed., *The Letters of Anthony Trollope* (London, 1951).

Briggs, Asa, 'Trollope, Bagehot and the English Constitution', *Cambridge Journal*, 5 (1952), 327–38.

Brown, Beatrice C., *Anthony Trollope* (London, 1950).

Clark, John W., *The Language and Style of Anthony Trollope* (London, 1975).

Cockshut, A.O.J., *Anthony Trollope: A Critical Study* (London, 1955).

Edwards, P.D., *Anthony Trollope: His Art and Scope* (London, 1978).

Escott, T.H.S., *Anthony Trollope: His Work, Associates and Literary Originals* (London, 1913).

Fredman, Alice G., 'Anthony Trollope', *Columbia Essays on Modern Writers*', (New York, 1971).

Hagan, John H., 'The Divided Mind of Anthony Trollope', *Nineteenth Century Fiction*, 14 (1959), 1–26.

Halperin, John, *Trollope and Politics: A Study of the Pallisers and Others* (London, 1977).

Harrison, Frederic, *Studies in Early Victorian Literature* (London, 1895).

Hennedy, Hugh L., *Unity in Barsetshire* (The Hague and Paris, 1971).

James, Henry, 'Anthony Trollope', *Partial Portraits* (London, 1888), pp. 97–133.

Ker, W. P., 'Anthony Trollope', *On Modern Literature*, ed. T. Spencer and J. Sutherland (Oxford, 1955), pp. 136–46.

Kincaid, James R., 'Bring Back *The Trollopian*', *Nineteenth Century Fiction*, 31 (1976), 1–14.

Kincaid, James R., *The Novels of Anthony Trollope* (Oxford, 1977).

McMaster, Juliet, *Trollope's Palliser Novels: Theme and Pattern* (London, 1978).

Mizener, Arthur, 'Anthony Trollope: The Palliser Novels', *From*

Jane Austen to Joseph Conrad, ed. R. C. Rathburn and M. Steinmann (Minneapolis, 1958), pp. 160–76.

Polhemus, Robert M., *The Changing World of Anthony Trollope* (Berkeley and Los Angeles, 1968).

Pollard, Arthur, *Anthony Trollope* (London, 1978).

Pollard, Arthur, *Trollope's Political Novels* (Hull, 1968).

Pope Hennessy, James, *Anthony Trollope* (London, 1971).

Ray, Gordon N., 'Trollope at Full Length', *Huntingdon Library Quarterly*, 31 (1968), 313–40.

apRoberts, Ruth, *Trollope: Artist and Moralist* (London, 1971).

Sadleir, Michael, *Trollope: A Commentary* (London, 1927).

Skilton, David, *Anthony Trollope and His Contemporaries* (London, 1972).

Smalley, Donald, ed., *Anthony Trollope: The Critical Heritage* (London, 1969).

Snow, C. P., *Trollope* (London, 1975).

Stebbins, L. P. and R. P., *The Trollopes: The Chronicle of a Writing Family* (London, 1946).

Terry, R. C., *Anthony Trollope: The Artist in Hiding* (London, 1977).

Thale, Jerome, 'The Problem of Structure in Trollope', *Nineteenth Century Fiction*, 15 (1960), 147–57.

Trollope, F. E., *Frances Trollope: Her Life and Literary Work* 2 vols (London, 1895).

Trollope, Thomas A., *What I Remember* 2 vols (London, 1887).

Walpole, Hugh, *Anthony Trollope* (London, 1928).

GENERAL STUDIES ON THE NOVEL

Booth, Wayne C., *The Rhetoric of Fiction* (Chicago, 1961).

Friedman, Alan, *The Turn of the Novel* (New York, 1966).

Graham, Kenneth, *English Criticism of the Novel 1865–1900* (Oxford, 1965).

Harvey, W. J., *Character and the Novel* (London, 1965).

Mendilow, A. A., *Time and the Novel* (London, 1952).

Miller, J. Hillis, *The Disappearance of God: Five Nineteenth-Century Writers* (Cambridge, Mass., 1963).

Miller, J. Hillis, *The Form of Victorian Fiction* (Notre Dame Indiana, 1968).

Praz, Mario, *The Hero in Eclipse in Victorian Fiction* tr. Angus Davidson, (London, 1956).

Scholes, Robert, and Kellogg, Robert, *The Nature of Narrative* (London, 1966).

Stang, Richard, *The Theory of the Novel in England 1850–1870* (London, 1959).

INDEX

Fictional characters are referred to in *italic*.